Weavings 2000

THE MARYLAND MILLENNIAL ANTHOLOGY

EDITED BY MICHAEL S. GLASER

International Standard Book Number: 0-938572-26-1
Library of Congress Control Number: 00-132290

First edition printed 2000
Printed in the U.S.A.

Typography and cover design by Cynthia Comitz, *In Support, Inc.*
Cover photography by Richard Smolko, *Potomac Photography*
Printing by George Klear, *Printing Press, Inc.*

This book was made possible by a generous grant from the
Maryland Commission for Celebration 2000

Published by Forest Woods Media Productions, Inc.
for the

Maryland Commission for Celebration 2000

For information contact the editor:
Michael S. Glaser
Weavings 2000
St. Mary's College of Maryland
St. Mary's City, MD 20686

www.maryland2000.org

Introduction

Each of us has memories of how the written word has woven itself into and around our lives. I remember Gilbert Byron, travelling as a Maryland Poet-in-the-Schools, telling children the story of how Marianne Moore kept re-writing her long poem "Poetry" (the one that begins "I too dislike it") until it was reduced to a very few lines that end, "Reading it, however...one discovers...in it...a place for the genuine."

I often think it is exactly that "genuine" response to human experience which makes literature so important. As Robert Coles suggests, good writing, like a good friend, serves to challenge as well as comfort us, it "offers us other eyes with which we might see and other ears with which we might make soundings." Literature provides windows inward and windows through which we might look at worlds that are different from our own. And often, literature enables us to see how the people who inhabit those worlds are not as radically different as we first imagined. Stories and poems provide us places wherein we can explore both our human connections as well as our distinct human otherness.

This anthology set out to be a kind of archival record – a millennial-ending gathering of work by writers who live in Maryland or who have passed through here on their journeys. One of the most exciting surprises we encountered in assembling the anthology was the realization of how many hundreds and hundreds of fine writers live in our state. We also experienced, from a new perspective, just how well our public and private schools, our community and four-year colleges, as well as our universities, are encouraging and nurturing the kind of reflective and artistic expression that we call "creative writing." While it quickly became apparent that this anthology could not possibly be all-inclusive, it has, nonetheless, sought to be representative of the wide variety of Marylanders who use language to give meaningful shape and expression to their experiences.

Many believe that it is the writer's work to live fully, to experience life as authentically as he or she can, and then to report out what the writer finds. It is my sense that the many and various voices in this anthology illustrate how that is done. Such an examination is, of course, not always comfortable because in looking at who we are, we do not always see what we would wish or hope for.

But almost always, the honesty and integrity of such examination enables us to better understand and sometimes, even, free ourselves from those perceptions, attitudes and experiences which entrap us. W. H. Auden may well have been right when he suggested that it is only because we can recognize the sound of the authentic voice that we are able to prevent others from reducing the human experience to so many political sound bites, catchy advertisers' slogans or sweet greeting card sentimentalities.

I hope you will find within the pages here, something of what I have found: a stirring of response to what is both genuine and authentic, food for the soul and spirit, challenges for the mind and heart, encouragement to be both more awake and more reflective.

Many people deserve appreciation for their help with this anthology. The editor would like to make special note of the following: Governor Parris Glendening who established the Maryland Commission for Celebration 2000; the chair of the Maryland Commission for Celebration 2000, the Honorable William Donald Schaefer; and the commission's vice chair, Dr. Jane Margaret O'Brien, president of St. Mary's College of Maryland. Also, Dr. Laraine Glidden, special assistant to the president at St. Mary's College, and chair of the education committee of the Maryland Commission for Celebration 2000. I also want to thank the entire staff of the commission whose work has nurtured and supported this project – especially Louise Hayman, executive director, and Alicia Moran, assistant director. Also to the members of the Maryland 2000 education committee who enthusiastically supported this anthology, and to the generous contributors to the Maryland Commission for Celebration 2000 who have underwritten this project, our appreciation and gratitude.

Additionally, recognition is due to a number of people whose hands-on efforts have literally given shape to this anthology: To Grace Cavalieri, always a guiding light for writers as well as for this anthology; to Kathryn Lange, associate editor, whose sensibilities inform this entire work; to the editorial staff and our executive assistant, Serena Graham, whose clear-sightedness, organization and hard work have enabled this anthology to emerge out of an exciting morass of manuscripts and good intentions; to Pamela Dunne and the Maryland State Arts Council; to Colie Ring, Gail Wood, and Janet Haugaard; to Allyson McGill, Peggy Marshall, and Cindy Comitz; to Wayne Karlin and Lucille Clifton, and to the many writers whose contributions to the 21ˢᵗ Literary Festival at St. Mary's in the summer of 1999 have been abstracted and edited to serve as the thoughtful "weavings" that I trust will give readers the option to pause and reflect in the process of reading through this anthology. And, finally, to the wonderful staff people at St. Mary's College of Maryland who, for 21 years, have worked tirelessly in support of the Literary Festival from which this anthology blossomed and in which its roots are centered.

There are many, many lives, seen and unseen, named and unnamed, which have directly contributed to this anthology, to the poems and stories herein, to the poets and writers whose work is recorded within. The song of one voice is connected to others in a hundred thousand ways. Even as we advance into the future, we carry with us the astonishingly complex composition of our past. It is, perhaps, this very complexity of weavings that enables a good poem or story, memoir or essay to profoundly touch our lives.

I like to think of this anthology as a gift to you, the reader, from the Maryland Commission for Celebration 2000 in recognition of the millennium. It is a proud affirmation of the art and spirit which exist in and are nurtured by the land, the water and the people who comprise our fair state.

Enjoy!

Michael S. Glaser
St. Mary's City
April, 2000

Contents

At the end of our bloody century, we might well pray that our country will turn more and more to the life of the spirit, and, when it does, a national archive of the spirit will be found in our poetry.

....*Roland Flint*

Poet Laureate of Maryland
at the turn of the millennium

A Major Work

Poems are hard to read
Pictures are hard to see
Music is hard to hear
And people are hard to love

But whether from brute need
Or divine energy
At last mind eye and ear
And the great sloth heart will move.

....*William Meredith*

The Owl

Dusk in suburbia lies like a pall
over the gabled roofs. We drive quickly
down Charles Street, heading home toward the city
when all at once what looks like a knitted shawl –
something grandma might wear, mouldy with fringe –
comes sailing straight for our car window,
until it's blown off course. We feel a twinge,
and before it roosts in the hemlock, know,
though we've never seen one live, that it's an owl,
too timid we've been told for our society.
He blinks, readjusts his monastic cowl,
gives what I can only call a lustful squeal,
then pushes back against the mournful tree,
seizing the mouse struck dumb beneath our wheel.

....David Bergman

Still Life

I must explain why it is that at night, in my own house,
Even when no one's asleep, I feel I must whisper.
Thoreau and Wordsworth would call it an act of devotion,
I think; others would call it fright; it is probably
Something of both. In my living-room there are matters I'd
   rather not meddle with
Late at night.

I prefer to sit very still on the couch, watching
All the inanimate things of my daytime life –
The furniture and the curtains, the pictures and books –
Come alive,
Not as in some childish fantasy, the chairs dancing
And Disney prancing backstage, but with dignity,
The big old rocker presiding over a silent
And solemn assembly of all my craftsmen,
From Picasso and other dignities gracing my walls
To the local carpenter benched at my slippered feet.

I find these proceedings
Remarkable for their clarity and intelligence, and I wish I
   might somehow
Bring into daylight the eloquence, say, of a doorknob.
But always the gathering breaks up; everyone there
Shrinks from the tossing turbulence
Of living,
A cough, a creaking stair.

Reed Whittemore

Thanksgiving Night: St. Michael's

Chesapeake Bay

A scarred night, fog, the sky a streaky white,
as we walk out, out on a finger of land
that points like a sign to World's End,
and step from land to water, the pier creaking
under us like the springs of an old bed.
We scare, by being here, a heron
from its hiding place; it changes itself
into blue smoke and wind and flies west
over the world's bright edge, leaving behind
an old ghost under the pier, the stiff ribs
of a skiff buried in black water. Eaten
by air, by water, each year there is less to it.
Behind us, a world too-human waits,
a crisscross of familiar streets and houses
painted with fresh paint, and lit storefronts,
their goods arranged in careful tiers and rows,
offering us the new, the young, the bright.
Skeletal night! Soon the tide will run out,
stranding the skiff, like a great beached fish,
in shallows, each bony rib countable, monstrous,
a feast of past, present, and future holidays
mingling, like wine in water, until all are one,
the dead, living, and not-yet-born gathered
around the great table to suck the sweet
marrow from the kill, as if there will always
be, for us, a tomorrow tomorrow.

....Elizabeth Spires

Looking for Divine Transportation

> "I heard the noise of their
> wings, like the noise of great
> waters...."
> -Ezekiel 1:24

I have wandered
into the Garden lured
by the fragrance and color

of delicate blossoms. Among
jabbering children speaking
innocent words I cannot repeat

and tragic characters in felt
hats, I search for those angels
who are wheels. With no visa

to be here, no encyclopedia
to guide me, I conjure
an image of you, let you

be my bible of common
sense: how to find my way
in; how to find the way out.

....Karren Alenier

Poem of the Mother

The heart goes out ahead
scouting for him
while I stay at home
keeping the fire,
holding the house down
around myself
like a skirt from the high wind.

The boy does not know
how my eye strains to make out
his small animal shape
swimming hard across the future
nor that I have strengthened myself
like the wood side of this house
for his benefit.

I stay still
so he can rail against me.
I stay at the fixed center of things
like a jar on its shelf
or the clock on the mantel
so when his time comes
he can leave me.

....Myra Sklarew

Lotus Pond

Like uncoiling cobras summoned by flute,
stems rise, roused out of muck
by music, by the chance,

here again, to ripen and swell
until each leaf unfolds,
purple side down, pins

its green heart open
on a mirror
with ten thousand others

on a sheen of water-silk.
This is how compassion grows:
out of the mud,

mottled by bruise.
And this is what it asks:
among ten thousand stems

intertwined and swaying
in underwater twilight,
who can trace which stalk

to which flower?
Who can say which heart is mine?
Which yours?

....Barbara Hurd

Meditation in Rock Creek Park

for my brother-in-law
Cal Revelle, 1952 - 1995

we sit along the forks
in this decaying log
great brown body
like a giant snake
sunning on the hill
we sit   our dogs circling us
their legs snatching at leaves
sit in a row the three of us
women   eyes level with the living tree-tops
faces turned to the smokey sun
the water below us throws out
dark sparks under the hushed light
the air is dense with
the red-brown perfume of dying leaves
and the dogs rustle as they settle down

my old one barks twice
then nestles near my feet
there is white along her jaw
the sockets of her eyes
as if the bones of her face
were beginning to shine through

they lie at angles to the log
the dog-bodies like warm breathing branches
their heads seem to float
their noses drifting halfway towards us
halfway where we're looking to

silence   my heart
pounds a circuit
that keeps me here for this brief time
keeps me anchored here
one of the breathers
in the leaf dust and liquid air

I want to take this moment
and mark it and send it to you
— somewhere
but where are you?
your bones go on dissolving in the earth
this same earth

as if you'd need this moment where you are
this second of daylight
no – your bones see light too
and you are not somewhere else
you are on this same earth
under this sunlight

if I took your bones
a few chips a handful of ashes
and threw them at the moon
you'd slide back down
you would not even leave this hemisphere
no one could fling you far enough
to touch the clouds

even our farthest satellite
circles within our pull

there is no escaping this universe

.....Ilona Popper

Montana Terrace
(progression to natural)

In my neighborhood
mothers were mountains
their jagged hearts climbed by children
& husbands seeking elevation

men, weak with selfish intentions
chipped away at their souls
blasting caps of hatred
shook their foundations

bearing the load of family
they carried a race on their backs
a steep ascent to destiny

In my neighborhood
mothers were mountains
i have seen them crumble

& become women.

& love them still.

.....Kenneth Carroll

The Miracle of Bubbles

A woman drives to the video store
to rent a movie. It is Saturday night,
she is thinking of nothing in particular,
perhaps of how later she will pop popcorn
or hold hands with her husband and pretend
they are still in high school. On the way home
a plane drops from the sky, the wing shearing
the roof of her car, killing her instantly.
Here is a death, it could happen to any of us.
Her husband will struggle the rest of his days
to give shape to an event that does not mean
to be understood. Since memory cannot operate
without plot, he chooses the romantic – how young
she was, her lovely waist, or the ironic – if only
she had lost her keys, stopped for pizza.

At the precise moment the plane spiraled
out of control, he was lathering shampoo
into his daughter's hair, blonde and fine
as cornsilk, in love with his life, his
daughter, the earth (for "cornsilk" is how
he thought of her hair), in love with the miracle
of bubbles, how they rise in a slow dance,
swell and shimmer in the steamy air, then
dissolve as though they never were.

....*Barbara Goldberg*

Stars

Imagine night
Without them:
Measureless dark
Forever unrelieved.

Who could believe
In purpose then;
Or ever wish
For anything but dawn?

Without stars,
Fire and lightning –
Ravenous, brief – would be
Life's natural metaphors.

Sunlight erases
Every possibility but one;
Swaddling us
In a blanket of watery blue.

Add a moon, and still
The never-ending
Round of change
Affords small comfort.

Beyond our power
To count and name,
Bright dots that challenge us
To draw connections,

The roof
All nations share,
The common field
Of every upturned eye,

Bridges of light
Even *our* folly cannot burn,
Glowing gems
That never waken greed,

Clock of caravans,
Mariner's guide, a prize
No one can tax,
Or steal,

Stars
Are all the proof we need
That some things worth creating
Do survive.

.....Lane Jennings

After Winter

He imagines his fingers
In the blacker loam
The lean months are done with,
The fat to come.

His eyes are set
On a brushwood-fire
But his heart is soaring
Higher and higher.

Though he stands ragged
An old scarecrow,
This is the way
His swift thoughts go

"Butter beans fo' Clara
Sugar corn fo' Grace
An' fo' de little feller
Runnin' space."

"Radishes and lettuce
Eggplants and beets
Turnips fo' de winter
An' candied sweets."

"Homespun tobacco
Apples in de bin
Fo' smokin' an' fo' cider
When de folks draps in."

He thinks with the winter
His troubles are gone;
Ten acres unplanted
To raise dreams on.

    The lean months are done with,
    The fat to come.
    His hopes, winter wanderers,
    Hasten home.

"Butter beans fo' Clara
Sugar corn fo' Grace
An' fo' de little feller
Runnin' space...."

                ....Sterling A. Brown

I grew up in three cultures simultaneously, but I learned to love and to take part in all three of those identities. When someone says I am half something, a half-breed, I say I am never half of anything. I am always a full Indian, a full Chicano, or a full American. Never part. My blood is not divisible.

....Edgar Silex

If we keep one thing from the twentieth century, perhaps it should be this realization: that we, all of us, are the beloved community to preserve. Too often we forget that. The business world tells us we are only worth our numbers: our age, our I.Q., and the potential profit of our ideas. We are reduced to our résumé. The media tell us we are mindless viewers, sometimes voyeurs, with a limited, predictable range of responses. And technology tells us that we can become obsolete as quickly as old software. But when the human spirit is pushed aside, it has the capacity to become more vital. That's why so many people are rediscovering poetry at schools and on the internet. They know on an instinctual, preintellectual level that poetry connects to our lost inner lives. They know that poetry speaks to the soul, not just the imagination. Poetry is the secular prayer for a people who seem to have few common anchors. As we begin the new millennium, we are not just standing in the doorway, but before a mirror. Who do we want to be? Literature helps us engage meaningfully in the search for answers to that question, and the best of today's poets and writers help by reminding us of what it means to be human. They speak with truth, and that alone is redemptive.

....Elizabeth Lund

Taken From the Top

Mountaintop, we scan the valley
  as God must, entrusting
  life to all directions;
  the dollhouse family
  in matchstick dwelling,
Horse and cow minute,
  cropping grass cocoon
  mid toy dog's scamper
  on the Earth balloon.
How miniscule is man,
  how fragile his frame –
  without his soul,
He and the ant selfsame.

....Marijane G. Ricketts

Scenes on the Road of Death

I. In the village

Hover over
the wooden hole
never sit
never

hawk eyes
watch carefully
each stranger

pull the children close

they burned the sacred ceiba
the trunk the limbs
my cousin's hut
my cousin

the dust left behind
gets in my face
my hair my teeth
my eyes

it is the clay oven
that cooks the food
we all eat.

II. The students

The van jerks wildly
to a stop
no place to hide
everyone sees her get sick

we will pretend
to look away, sadness
choking our hearts
collective relief

living things disappeared

clear cut
corn refuses to grow
the soil remembers
a different story

roots of giant trees
holding down the underworld
cradling the bones
of our history lesson

our driver is nervous
we cannot travel
this road
at night.

III. Lone bird

It is too quiet
i saw the men come
to make an example
of their brothers and sisters

i saw the bulldozers
scrape the earth of green
to plant the red clay
i warned them

my voice was too small

i still sing
in the new field
but no one
answers.

IV.   Spirit of the dead

November 1
colorful paper designs
newly painted stones
call me back

a special meal
served with hope
invisible, taken away
like their pain

for a day
the great family
beyond the village
unknown to the young

filled empty lungs
with moist forest air
the first and last breath
repeated.

...Jeanne Fryberger Vote

First Days in a World

for Caroline

> Like hearing parents, some deaf parents also
> expect to have a child who is the same as
> themselves...[But in the case of deaf parents
> of hearing children,] how is it possible that
> parent and child from two such different
> worlds can meet?
> -Paul Preston, *Mother Father Deaf*

Right now, of everything that's visible
And yet means nothing, this shy man, your father
Deaf since birth, who's watched you for an hour,
May be most important. He's been told
His twin daughters, weeks premature, can hear,
But can't believe it yet, not till he sees
Some sign in your response beyond the glass
Dividing him from you. He taps the window,
Sensing its vibration; taps again,
And all the babies twitch. How small your hands
Are, flexing while your sister cries; and now
He knows – elated, saddened – *Time to go*,
The nurse touches his arm, and so he does,
Though when he finds your mother still asleep,
He'll have nowhere to go except the lobby
Or outside, to smoke...For you, whose newborn
Hands, short-fingered, dense with lines, close now
And fall down at your side, the world is what
Rocks you within its hum, all cries except
Your own drowned out, a bright machinery
That warms you in its shell. You want so much
Just to be held these first days in a world
More like his than you'll ever know again.

.....Ned Balbo

Already the Heart

The spinal cord blossoms
like bright, bruised magnolia
into the brainstem.
            And already the heart
in its depth – who could assail it?
Bathed in my voice, all branching
and dreaming. *The flowering
and fading* – said the poet –
come to us both at once.
Here is your best self,
and the least, two sparrows
alight in the one tree
of your body.

....A. V. Christie

Song of Herself

She sings a song
from the other room
and the notes and melody and the river of it
stream in to where I am,

where this person who was I is,
an I changed.

She's an orange, she's a sky,
a blue ball on the beach,
an annunciation.

She's this new song –
the notes fall and rise, warm and ticklish.

It was the sound of her, first,
like a *New Yorker* cartoon I saw once:
a *waah* from a bassinet, as if
the bassinet were alive, speaking, God's voice,
the joy the joy the joy
of sudden sound. (In the cartoon
it's funny. It is. It is funny.)

Her voice. Her small throat extends up
and her small mouth turns into an O and then –

her arms pull up and she pushes her hands
below her chin
and with her black eyes –
more distinct all the time, as if she is
pulling up from the soul of the world
to her own individual soul, and she's

so assuredly her own by now – she holds me,

she brings me. She brings me, the new me,
to the music hall. It is. It is!

....*Aurelie Sheehan*

34

Into the Orchard

Stooping for an apple,
I see the shadow of a horse;
in his mane, angels.
Fruit, limb, tree: a trinity.
It is time to taste
the ripened body.

In every fruit I see angels,
food for my mortal body,
communion with trinity.
I shine the ripest apple,
leave the core for a horse.
His body is what I taste.

In the cider heap, Christ's body,
Eve's sin, the apple.
What I desire I cannot taste:
to be Mary, on a horse,
voice lifted to the trinity,
praising the bruise-free skin of angels.

I have a taste
for angels.
I see a child on a horse,
the limbs of his body
curl up into stem and apple,
one with the trinity.

In my hand, the smallest trinity:
peel, stem, seed — taste
of a newly fallen apple,
food and drink of angels.
I eat the fruit's white body,
hear the whinny of a horse.

A pale woman on a white horse
is filled with the trinity;
the child within her, a body
feeding on the taste
of Eden, the sound of angels
among branches, seeds in the apple.

My body, too, feeds on that taste.
I walk past the horse, singing to the trinity,
like an angel praising the apple.

....*Elizabeth Lund*

Bee

For once I was not bent
on denying the worst scenario
but listened to the bee
get louder as it came closer.
I was still as the rumble moved
into my chest and the machinery
of its wings passed over.

*

The bee kept changing direction, mid-air
and the sound diminïshed or drew close randomly.
I've seen the brightest yellow flicker
do the same in a wet, green field
– take one sip, reverse itself
and look for some fresh thing because
it so loved the idea of abundance.

*

But I was only part of the abundance.
And who else would I be
so adorned, but clearly
an attractive thing to it,
a singular sweetness.
I mean, I was willing
to think like an ornament.

*

Then I saw myself as I was –
not nearly what it wanted.
I did not grow, like the rose,
dangerous and inviting
steps to my heart and my heart
was not perfect – hidden,
dusty and small.

*

In place of what it wanted,
I would do. And I saw
my two wild arms
in the air, waving,
not knowing how to say
I was more than that,
in its language.

.....*Lia Purpura*

Take Hold

If there is nothing
before you, take hold
of it. You may be fortunate
or not. Place it deep
in your pocket regardless.
It is a possession
as no other.

When you are to leave and
have made all your
preparations; when you
are ordered to declare all
your possessions, reach in
to the dark pocket.

This is a symbol
traveler, a parable
perhaps. Nothing
is as whole as the space
in the air
you pass through.
And it is yours. If
you will take hold of it.

....Merrill Leffler

we are running

running and
time is clocking us
from the edge like an only
daughter.
our mothers stream before us,
cradling their breasts in their
hands.
oh pray that what we want
is worth this running,
pray that what we're running
toward
is what we want.

.....Lucille Clifton

Harriet Tubman Said...

There are many kinds of being scared:
hiding out with snakes in a swamp,
praying in a whisper so low the Lord
strains to hear. And in morning light
all gold and flashy, you trample down
marshweed beside the road, shivering at
every bird call, or you hold on
to some long, way back love, wishing
against all odds your name will come up
on his lips. Sometimes it's a brief glimpse
of old square-toed death, reared-up
on his hind legs, waiting.

My train only moves one way and it's up
a mountain. You left fear standing
in a field with a whip. He was your
running start. Now he's sniffing around,
licking your heels, tasting your sweat.
You turn and I see him behind your eyes.
He suits you fine 'cause he's all you had
for so long. But I'll tell you this,
you can't go back. Fear will never be
so close to you as this cold iron finger
I hold in your ear. You can only die once.
You can die now, or you can be free.

....Maxine Clair

Blue-Green Spirit

Oh Dream Wanderer
with your message stick
with your rooster crowing,

Where is the voice I spoke
after I was dead
before I was born?

How much has been left by the wayside?

If every dream were a tattoo
how would I look?

Would I start loving my skin
turning in the light
holding up my arm to understand
what each flower means?

They say because the female bird
can't sing
she flies only during Summer in Sweden,

Oh no, listen,
she is connected to the divine and
sings of her taste for life and death,

She sings until heard,
it is the voice we share where
nothing is lost.

...Grace Cavalieri

The Cheer

reader my friend, is in the words here, somewhere.
Frankly, I'd like to make you smile.
Words addressing evil won't turn evil back
but they can give heart.
The cheer is hidden in right words.

A great deal isn't right, as they say,
as they are lately at some pains to tell us.
Words have to speak about that.
They would be the less words
for saying *smile* when they should say *do*.
If you ask them *do what?*
they turn serious quick enough, but never unlovely.
And they will tell you what to do,
if you listen, if you want that.

Certainly good cheer has never been what's wrong,
though solemn people mistrust it.
Against evil, between evils, lovely words are right.
How absurd it would be to spin these noises out,
so serious that we call them poems,
if they couldn't make a person smile.
Cheer or courage is what they were all born in.
It's what they're trying to tell us, miming like that.
It's native to the words,
and what they want us always to know,
even when it seems quite impossible to do.

.....William Meredith

What matters? A letter arrives: You don't know me. Today
we buried my dear friend. Nothing could console me. Tonight
by accident I picked up your book and read "Things are Still
Coming Ashore." You have helped me grow. I wanted you to know.

What matters? At Iowa, Robert Frost told us: the poem begins
in delight and ends in wisdom. The figure is the same for love.

When I was nine, Eliot's Prufrock said to me "Let us go then,
you and I, when the evening is spread out against the sky
like a patient etherized upon a table" and I never recovered.

That was what the world was about! Going with the sights and
sounds of words, words. And the lines began to sing themselves
to me and still do. They keep coming on and I try to get them
down as fast as I can.

What matters? Love and the poems.

....Ann Darr

Charity

The sun rises for the dogs who are blinded
by light. One day strides with its long legs
into the next. Charity works in the passing.

And the woman is grateful for her heart which
lets her down, thankful for foxglove blooming,
taller than her hopes, in the spotted light beyond

the wall. A brown toad pulses, a worm makes
good dirt – a woman takes her heart for a walk.
All light will rise like heat; shadow will save her

– even a poppy guards its purple cunning. Such
heart beats there – good darkness, footsteps and
blunders, a blind dog finding its long, late way.

....Renée Ashley

The Cat's Eye in the Fell's Point section of Baltimore was owned by an ex-biker named Kenny Orey, a tough-as-nails character rumored to have been a gun-runner for the Provos. At twenty-five, Kenny looked fifty. Ask anyone who knew him. Kenny lived hard. He used to sit at the bar drinking beer and snorting coke through a Vicks nasal inhaler. On his birthday, the employees would carry him into the bar in a coffin, in a mock funeral. Why they did this, I don't know. The coffin remained the rest of the year in the tiny, filthy store-room in the back, which also served as the band room. Kenny dropped dead in his early thirties, I think from a heart attack. My impression is that he never intended to live long. That was about ten years ago.

I always liked Kenny. He looked pretty scary – he had squinty, mean eyes, bad skin, and greasy red hair – but he seemed like a decent guy. The Cat's Eye operated like something scripted for a bad sit-com, and that's what endeared it to its patrons. Kenny or his second-in-command – a dead ringer for Abraham Lincoln who, in fact, supposedly made good money as a Lincoln impersonator – would quite regularly double-book the place. So we would show up to play five minutes before some other band would arrive. Or we'd be setting up and another group would enter with their instruments and equipment. Kenny always handled these situations with Solomonic adroitness. He'd tell us to play only one set, for example, then pay us for the entire night. Musicians salute that kind of behavior in bar owners.

It's difficult, really, to convey a sense of the strangeness of the Cat's Eye. This was a place unlike all others. When you entered the Cat, you stepped into a bizarre realm where the rules of normal life simply didn't apply. Where your usual expectations were no use as a guide to this weird terrain. Lugging the owner around in a coffin? Standard procedure. Honest Abe himself sliding mugs of beer down the bar? Business as usual.

Across from the Cat the waters of Baltimore harbor lapped at the street, and in the bar hung a sign proclaiming that "The Only Thing We Overlook Is The Harbor."

I heard that once Kenny fired an automatic weapon from the second story of the Cat, scattering some irritating adversaries who had gathered on the street below. If the Cat's Eye often seemed cartoonish, the danger it attracted felt very real.

One night at closing time, Kenny couldn't dislodge a few of the old drunks still sitting at the bar. We were already on the street, loading up the van for the trip back to DC. I watched as Kenny came out the front door, closed it, lit several smoke bombs, opened the door, and tossed them into his establishment, yelling "fire!" Men stumbled out into the night, befuddled, drunk, adjusting their clothes, somewhere inside dimly aware of danger and the need to flee. Another night, as we were on the street packing up early because of a double-booking, about twenty-five Hell's Angels, former associates of Kenny's, screeched up to the front door on their bikes, looking angry and armed. I remember watching them march into the Cat and thinking Thank You God for placing me out here and them in there.

I don't believe in God, even though I thanked him. Sometimes I think I could go for the "higher power" notion from AA. They say you can interpret the higher power loosely, so that it could be your conscience or your love for music, for example. But making the higher power so much a matter of per-sonal definition robs it of authority. There's a huge gap separating my con-science from the Unmoved Mover.

Then, sometimes, I feel myself lunging toward belief. I contemplate that nanosecond right after the Big Bang and get lost in the icy vast timelessness, the overwhelming dark measurelessness of everything. Sometimes the proofs for the existence of God appear to be endless, abundant, undeniable. But most of the time, I don't even think about it, even though I can taste my own fear some days. Other days it all just seems ridiculous – a relentless spectacle of fat men, still alive, being carried around in coffins. In Baltimore at the Cat's Eye, I felt I was adrift in the distant past, so medieval did it all seem.

But more than anything else, it was the dogs that amazed me. From the bandstand at the Cat, you faced the bar, with the bartender facing back at you, and the patrons on their stools with their backs to you. My first night playing there, I was absent-mindedly scanning the room. Most of the stools were taken. There sat a woman talking to a man, then a man alone, smoking a cigarette, then – what? Yes, it was. On the stool sat a dog, who came to roughly the same height as the humans. He looked right at home. I half expected him to flick a cigarette at the ashtray and sip at a beer. I continued scanning. Another woman, a man, a man, another dog. Yes, the dogs were part of the mix all right. Why not dress them up in hats and jackets and teach them to yowl out "Danny Boy"?

Later that first night, I was hungry and the kitchen was long closed. I noticed a few nut machines near the bandstand, offering peanuts and cashews, a quarter per handful. So I got change and went over to the machines and dropped a quarter in the cashew slot. As the nuts tumbled into my cupped palm, I felt a hand on my chest and turned my head. A large dog was staring into my eyes, standing on his hind legs, with one paw planted on my chest. In this upright position, he was close to my height. He clearly wanted a few nuts. His look was so intelligent, so clear. It seemed to me he said, with his eyes, "Hey, chief, help us out with a few cashews." I gave him a couple of nuts.

On summer nights, I'd sit out front on our breaks and watch the moon glinting on the water, with that feeling you have, especially when you're young, that your life is a still point in the whirl of chaos, and that you will always be right there, watching the smoke rise from your cigarette, meditating on the ideal, the golden city of your purest dreams.

.... *Terence Winch*

Poetry Sends Her Love

Suddenly I'm helping
to pack Poetry's car.
And good riddance I'm saying,
*What have you ever
done for me?* Poetry
is driving away, waving
farewell, leaving me
to my life.
A few months go by.

I open the refrigerator
door to find
some peaches: yellow and red,
each gathered square
and greenly toward its stem.
Against my fingers, a seam
runs down the center:
plush skin. I'm holding
one of the peaches
and standing there.

A few days later,
I get the letter. She hasn't
forgotten. Still eloquent,
everything spelled correctly,
a light perfume on fine bond in her
inimitable calligraphy:
Beloved, it says,
*everything has its beauty, you
as well, its form
inside that rises
to the skin. Did you get
those peaches?*

.....*Sam Schmidt*

Hope

For all the cooks
Who in the early morning
Especially the cold mornings
Turn grills on and get batter ready
For them and
For hillsides
Particularly the ones
That slope up just enough
To bring on panting
But not stopping
For them as well and
For wash cloths
The most helpful being cotton and
Old ones
For all of them
Mostly because they are sleepy
In a rousing sort of way.

.....Hiram Larew

Our Mother Serves Glamour for Breakfast

"Glamour isn't everything."
Judy Garland declares from the TV screen.
Our mother says, "Don't believe her,"
Our mother could have been in show business
if she hadn't gotten stage fright so bad
each spring at dance recital.
She sings and shuffles off to Buffalo
in her fluffy pink slippers,
red toenails poking out.
My sister and I chew our Wheaties,
wonder who will get the prize in the box.

Our mother scours the kitchen sink,
buffs the metal cabinets
til their chrome shines
like the kitchen floor.
She sings, "Oh What a Beautiful Morning"
and all the songs from Oklahoma
as she mops dust out the door
of our project apartment.

I clear away the breakfast bowls
as she sits my sister on the table for therapy.
Her strong hands mold
my sister's crooked feet,
bend my sister's limp legs
back and forth
back and forth trying to wake the muscles.

My sister is four.
She wants to be a ballerina.
Our mother says yes.
She will sew a tutu with the colors of the rainbow.
She sings to her,

"You must have been a beautiful baby,
cause Baby, look at you now"
I tap-dance my Ginny dolls across the linoleum.

There was another man my mother
might have married,
She might have got a job in Europe
if my father's eyes had not been so blue.
Before she met our father,
she got her picture on the front page
outside the theater, the day she skipped school
to see Frank Sinatra.

Now she's off to clean the bathroom.
On her knees she scrubs the tub and toilet,
the white powder turns to blue.
"Put your dreams away for another day,
darling...." Her voice echoes against pink ceramic.
My sister and I hum along.
We agree.
Glamour is everything.

.....*Laura K. Lynds*

A House is a Story

To begin, there is a room
so full of people it takes you
most of your life to enter.
For years you didn't try, only peering
sideways through the locked glass doors.
There is your breath, soft on the pane.
You pause, try to change, or shed the invisible
face of your inheritance. You reach
for any hand to carry you in.
When someone finally shrugs and steps aside,
you slip by with your eyes down –
one of the tasks agreed on
silently when they built this house
against the rain, against a voice
rising inside, making room.

....Dan Johnson

Driving on the Beltway

On the Beltway
I miss the earthliness.
Instead of the buoyant
steadiness

of forsythia's yellow, expectancy
of apple tree buds breathing
their white insides open
in fragrance, the coolness

of tulip leaves slowly unwrapping
in wisps of laughter,

I feel the push

of passing cars, the uneven
pavement, borders
of broken lines,
concrete barriers. While I count

the exits, the minutes crawl
along my spine, deposit lead
in my thighs. I long
for a whiff of chocolate mulch

freshly piled around the trees.
To stop.
To touch the porous skin.
To be touched.

.....Danuta E. Kosk-Kosicka

Maundy Thursday

You don't want to hear this old story, green as it is. Yes,
the early sun. Girls in pinafores snap sticks on the cobbled
street, their hair even shines – this light after a storm
stuns something in all of us. Water rushes the mill trench,
long heavy ribbons. Geese sleep tucked in shade. And the corn
rail stands so high. Why do we want what we have as we leave it?
Why then go at all? Looking South now, from this hill, nothing
but sea after sea, a possible circumnavigation of swollen water
in one state or another from here to here again. And what?
The newly turned earth beside you is not enough? The pair
of white butterflies reminding you *go barefoot*? Didn't Spring
always find you perched in some high sunned place? Like this?

.....*Robin Holland*

The Sunflowers

Acre by acre, the sunflowers
shed their golden manes and
turn their heads away from the sun
grieving the end of summer.

In June they grew thick as a forest,
erect with the thick sap swelling up
in them almost to bursting point.

Now their heads bend to the earth
from which they rose, each withered stem
the ghost of a spent summer pleasure –

The morning we ran
the whole way to the cape
as the sun lifted like a
flamingo's pretty head
on the turquoise horizon,
How the fishermen we met
along the way spoke humbly
to you as though a god had
stopped by to chat and touch
the silver bellies of their fish
bringing the evening catch
back to life.

    The days we stripped
and chased each other, bronze
and alabaster far out into the
sapphire swell of the Black Sea.

The animal joy.
The silky pleasure.
The surf, the shower,
full moon, foam, your
shining body – how often
did your touch bring me
to the bursting point, death
after sweet little death, now
gone, all gone, summer gone,
you gone, relentless farewell
of the railway clatter
dovijdane, dovijdane, dovijdane
as my train makes its slow way
across the breast of Bulgaria
where the sunflowers stand
weeping in the fields, their
seeds falling like black tears
to the black earth, where
they must plant their grief
in the end and go to bed
like good children. Throughout
the frozen winter they must
dream of the sun, radiant
as the joy that filled our days
the summer long so they
may flower again when the
spring first thaws the fields
with her sweet breath and
bid them rise, rise – endless
as my summer love.

....*Richard Harteis*

Waking

for Mackenzie, age 2

She wakes in her new bed, calling out my name.
As my head rises from the pillow, she smiles.
She asks me if she can wake up now,
as if to make sure it is morning
and not dark anymore.

She climbs out of her bed and into mine,
places her yellow knitted blanket on my lap
and rests her head on my knee.

I gaze at her, trying to imagine
what is going through her mind.
I think she is a wonder.

She asks for a drink of water
and we go to the kitchen
where I pour her a cup.

She carefully climbs onto her chair
at the table, and drinks
while I stare at her in amazement
watching how carefully
she sips and puts the cup down –
every movement distinct, important.
Then softly, she reaches her hand to mine.

On this cold morning, I am filled
with warmth. I smile,
learning more every day
what is truly important.

.... Eva Glaser

Lies

Lies are the worst thing I know.
Lies are like a bouncing ball
that goes on and on.

Before you know it
the ball will stop
and just be waiting there
like an endless pit
or a mom's disappointed stare.

.... Tyler Anderson

*The writer as a recorder of a kind of personal
history serves a very important function as we
move into a new century, a new millennium.
There are ways, I think, in which by understanding what happened to us in the past, we
can understand what might happen in the
future. I see the writer as a kind of savior. In
many ways, that's the most important function
of the writer — as the savior of the past, as the
person who builds a bridge and a connection
between the past and the future.*

....Maria Mazziotti Gillan

Marquee

When does the applause for fall's splendor
Become the grey silence of winter?
I try each year, but can never catch the last act.

Each time I am sure I can see the warm yellow stage,
The final red curtain,
The last leaf fall
Before the lights go down and the cold comes.

But they finish while I am on the road,
Moving through a colorful blur,
Driving too fast to get home.

Where is fall's schedule posted?
How can I be on time?
If the signs were left up,
At least I could read what I missed,

But as soon as the season is over
They are taken down, thrown away. Then
Winter posts its own coming attractions
And advance tickets for spring.

.....Kate Richardson

Chartres Cathedral

You will see Chartres Cathedral, they said, eight
or nine miles from the town. And so we did,
Windshield wipers sweeping at
the flashing rain. Wheat stacked each side

of the road. Out of mist, two spires rose.
Peguy had walked this way: one pilgrim more
in centuries of pilgrims. We tried to teach our eyes
to hold the ancient church. But the town was there

and we in the narrow street before the Royal Door.
Blue windows of Chartres, and God creating man
in joyful stone; gargoyle and buttress – clear
in sunlight after rain. What we had known

we realized: glass is flame, stone
is story; love is reaped where love was sown.

....Sr. Maura Eichner

A number of years ago, I had a dream. The car I was driving had in its trunk an art treasure, something wrapped in black velvet.* I had been given instructions to drive to the wettest fringes of town, to carry the treasure through twilight muck, to lean over and press it into the trembling ground until the earth redraped its covers and buried it completely. I never knew what the treasure was, but the image of its burial is clear to this day – that lowering of something that could keep for years if need be, rocking and swaying two feet deep in the dappled soddenness of bog. It was the kind of dream you cannot shake off, that clings to the skin. You notice it at the oddest moments, your arm vaguely green as you reach through a patch of morning sun for the Cheerios box on the kitchen table. Or in those moments, barefoot in the garden, when your toes disappear in a profusion of potato plants.

Like most everything from glaciers and meringue to humans and their relationships, from a distance a bog looks solid. From the air over Cranesville Swamp what you see in autumn is plush umber dotted with tufts of cotton grass, acres of nap rubbed the wrong way, the fuzzed yarns of velvet gold. It looks firm enough, as if you could, in an emergency, throttle your engines back, lower the wing flaps and landing gear, and ease your small plane down in this large clearing between forested ridges of western Maryland, bumping and skidding across a runway of dying weeds and hardened mud. It's an illusion, like the solidity of glaciers. Once in Alaska, I made my way, gingerly, across a glacier, astonished at how hard I had to work to avoid millwells and tunnels, crevasses large enough for people and dogsleds to fall into, rubble and rock fragment, the debris of high-country canyons. I thought about John Muir galloping and yahooing his way across glaciers like a big-pawed puppy skidding over hardwood floors. Wasn't he afraid of falling in? Doesn't intimacy always reveal the pores, the loosely woven, the invitation to go below, the way the bog invites, gurgling and swaying and rearranging itself around your by-now-somersaulted plane, its tousled layers of sphagnum and cranberry rising over your upside-down windshield?

The psyche of Western cultures is dampened by bog monsters and the swamp lights of aliens. In high school English classes all across the country, we follow Beowulf down into the murky, demon-infested waters of Grendel's lair. We have grown up with the Swamp Thing lurching through gnarled cypress trees, its breath like wind from Hades, with the Creature of the Black Lagoon, with bog elves and flickering lights luring innocent humans to live burials in quaking mires. Even our language is soaked with its doom: we are "bogged down" in too much work, "swamped" by debts, "mired" in triviality. Once I visited an elementary school and had my students writing poems about landscapes. One of them wrote about swamps, about green ooze, about wishing he could fling a bully cousin into the middle of a burpy crypt of slippery slime. When he read his poem to his classmates, they squirmed in their seats and cried "Oh, yuck!" and reveled in the image of the brute up to his ears in muck, algae dripping from his pimples. What is evidently worse punishment than being stripped, desert-style, of unnecessary accouterments, as Moses and his people were, is being immersed in all of them. All the endless variety of bullfrogs, bog orchids, swamp beacons, skunk cabbage. All the sinking, slurping, lumpy conglomeration of mud and plant and water. This is an onslaught on the senses, where even what you stand on is solid one minute and liquid the next. The Western mind loves lines and categories, the neat logic of syllogisms, clear and indisputable as Mount Hood against a summer sunset. Meanwhile, in the slow backwater, in pools between scum-slicked swamps, above the bowl-shaped leaves of *Nelumbo luteu* floats the American lotus, the yellow blossom of the water lily, upon which the Buddha sits, contemplating the paradox voiced by a zookeeper in Dublin who, when asked for the secret of his unusually successful breeding of lions, answered, "Understanding lions," and, when asked for the secret of understanding lions, replied, "Every lion is different."

I love the names of swamps, how they are as varied as their origins: Great Dismal, Four Holes, Big Thicket, Mingo, LaRue, Callahan, and Honey Island. Some of them oozed into being in high shallow bowls as glaciers withdrew their icy fingers. Some of them formed as the ancient Atlantic slid off an inland continental shelf and land rose behind it and rainwater flushed salt out of the pocket left behind. Concerning the origins of Lake Drummond in the center of Dismal Swamp, some scientists speculate about the impact of a giant meteor. Others suggest that the swamp might have been formed by hundreds of years of a giant underground peatburn. I like this theory. It reminds me of a friend I used to know who tried working as a hairstylist, who spent his days clipping and curling and chatting. All the while his underground was smoldering. You could feel it if you got too close, layers and layers of compressed decay smoking and smoldering, collapsing into themselves like hot coals into ash. He liked to read Goethe, who praises what longs to be burned to death. But imagine the surprise if, after years of such smoldering, what happens next is not the great transformative fire but an underground collapse, a sinking

depression, slow filling with rainwater and nearby flooding rivers, the ignomini-
ous creep of moss and duckweed and the gradual silence of the swamp.

Having opted today for the boardwalk that crosses Cranesville, I feel con-
spicuous, too upright in this bog where almost everything else spreads sideways.
Sphagnum moss stretches its vast network of cells, living and dead, out across
the acres. It reaches from the edge of the pond in toward the middle. It will
someday take over. It creeps like a thick raft, its underbelly always dying, its
sun-soaked surface a dense sponge of pale green tentacled stems. The term
quaking bog comes from this characteristic sponginess – you can actually step
onto the sphagnum, jump up and down, and feel the ground sway under your
feet. It would be, I suppose, a way to give a chicken like me some semblance of
surfing – holding the feet steady, keeping knees bent and flexible, riding the
waves of sphagnum and hair-cap moss. I step back onto the boardwalk and lie
down on warm planks to watch the size-nine boot-shaped pools of black water
I have left in the bog disappear. I stare and stare. I want not just the overall
effect of the vanished but the cause and exact moment of change. I want to
see this clump of bog moss, that strand of sphagnum straighten and stretch,
link tentacles with another, fill in the footprint. But all I get are the quick
sparkles of sunlight as plant and water rearrange themselves. If I look away,
even for five seconds, and then back, I can see change, how the instep and heel
have filled in. But if I keep my eyes glued to the footprint, nothing seems to
happen.

It is impossible to spend any time belly down on the boardwalk, face to face
with that wobbly cover, and not eventually reach over and push your fingers in.
We are drawn to what's below. From the safety of whatever boardwalks we
have chosen, we linger at the edges, testing the mire with the tips of galoshes, a
long stick, a hand. Do we dare? Do we dare? When I was ten, I loved the
scabs on my legs. I scratched mosquito bites until they bled and walked around
all summer, lifting the hard crusty edges of scabs, the way I might have lifted
manhole covers in a city street. I loved the moistness underneath. I loved
imagining my shins dotted with shallow ponds the size of lentils, complete with
sedgy fringes and the chorus of spring peepers, the possibility of lowering
myself into a labyrinth. I lived, at that time, in a neighborhood whose northern
edge abutted a small swamp. I remember that swamp only in winter. I remember the icy hummocks we used as hassocks, half-sitting, half-leaning against
them when we bent over to tie our skates on, the still, shallow water solidly
frozen and skimmed with white, the swamp edges solid as playground benches.
A swamp that to my child's mind had no depth, only white flatness, a slick

surface to glide across. But when geese flew north and the ice thinned until blackwater showed through again, the swamp dropped out of my psyche. In my mind, I must have pleated the land there, drawn one side of the neighborhood up against the field on the other side and left the swamp dangling in the fold underneath.

Once I walked all afternoon in a bog high on Meadow Mountain. I was headed north, skirting and crossing, dipping into and out of the red plush of rugosa sphagnum. I was thinking about the German poet Rainer Maria Rilke and how, on the page, his poems look like poems. They have titles and they sit still when you close the book and return it to the shelf. But his language is more like a steep slope. Or like the well on my grandmother's farm. If you lean over far enough, you fall in, and once you do, that tremendous thirst begins. I was thinking about those lines of his, in which he feels himself pushing through solid rock. I show him this bog. I want to know if he's ever been in such a place, if his dark god with its webbing of roots began in a swamp, the way Horus did after Isis hovered above her dead husband in a swamp until out of that ooze enough rose up that she conceived him. I show him the Nile goose, that swamp bird who laid the cosmic egg. He leads me out of the swamp and into the flintlike layers that surround him, where "everything close to my face is stone." I want him to practice what he knows about hunger, to begin wherever he is, pressing his teeth into the rock beneath his lips, his tongue against the ore, to see what happens when darkness meets an appetite. He wants me to know what makes us all small. He hands me a stone. This is your life, he says, sometimes a stone deep inside you, sometimes a star.

One summer I became obsessed with finding the edge of a nearby bog. I hiked its perimeter with a long stick, jabbing it into the muck every ten feet or so. I spent a week in a seminar, learning how the government delineates wetlands. We learned about obligate hydrophytes, facultative plant life, about hydrology and soil samples and soil maps. The government's guide to finding the edge of a swamp is fifty pages long, complete with graphs and soil maps you need a magnifying glass to decipher. We spent hours mucking in the field with spades and buckets and Munsell soil color charts, the same bog I had crisscrossed with my long stick of maple. At the end, I understood how trying to define a bog is like trying to put a neatly folded shadow into a dresser drawer. What and where the bog is is inseparable from who we are. And who we think we are not. In the Cameroons, the shadow is sacred. Its length is a sign of power. Its absence is a sign of death. Our efforts to define these places are efforts to separate ourselves from them, from their shifting boundaries, their reminders of decay, where what sways beneath the feet is both itself and its opposite at the same time.

From the Cranesville boardwalk today, I push my fingers down into the bog as deep as I can. They disappear. There's no telling what they will encounter down there or what will spy my five-pronged flesh shoved through the baroque ceiling of its world, groping around in dark rooms below. When I can push no further, it's not because my fingers have hit solid ground. What stops them in a net whose weave gets tighter and tighter the deeper you go. Down there, out of sight, my stubby fingers try tearing holes in the net, spreading apart the woof and the warp enough to push an index finger further. I can't. I'm down three inches and can go no more. I pull my fingers out, the bog slurping and slavering, and insert a pointed stick half an inch in diameter. Standing on the edge of the boardwalk, I lean on it, pushing slowly down. I am a medieval surgeon probing the body of a patient. The stick goes down three inches, ten, twenty. Two feet down, it breaks off and I almost fall in. The water slips over its fractured tip, the sphagnum straightens, and the buried half disappears.

A man I know, a wetlands expert, once sank to his chest in a bog more loosely woven than this one, sank until his toes were five feet under, his heart nestled among the green shoots of cotton grass in a place known as Hammel's Glade. He said it was good, good to stand there with the earth up to his shoulders, sepia pools and sedges drifting in waves. Thoreau would have loved him, both of them at home in the swamps, both aware that in between the big events, the graduations, weddings, births, and death, lies a damp profusion of chaos and contentment. Thoreau says, "I derive more of my subsistence from the swamps which surround my native town than from the cultivated gardens in the village. There are no richer parterres to my eyes." Perhaps it is, as Thoreau says, the tenderness of swamps that draws us. Here are places in the earth you can enter without backhoe and chisels and dynamite, without ropes and helmets and lanterns. All it takes is a step off the edge, the willingness to imagine being buried alive, which is how the wetlands man described it, standing in Hammel's Glade while the bog floated its beds under his chin. And that's the rub. Anticipating death is hard enough, but how to go at it in slow motion, immersed in the decay of last century's plant life with nothing to do but chronicle the way one's bones become almost visible beneath flesh?

The man got out, of course, had lunch somewhere, went home. Not everyone does. Bogs are famous burial grounds. There are stories in Ireland, in Germany and Denmark and England, of hundreds of men, women, and children buried in bogs, some of them lured into the misty muck by flickering lights, by bog elves, some of them minus their ears, lips, the skin torn off their backs. The highly acidic water in a bog means that the usual microorganisms that decompose a body are all but absent. Add in the very cold water and what you have are ideal conditions for preservation. In 1450, German peasants found the upright body of a man hundreds of years old buried to his neck in a bog. Concerned about a proper interment, the peasants went to the local priest, who forbade his burial in the churchyard. The reason? The priest believed that the man had been lured into the mire by bog elves. Evidently anyone susceptible to such spirits wasn't worthy of the sacraments. But maybe there's something else here. Maybe the priest saw the man as someone who had stood too long in the doorway between two worlds. Who knows what his death was like? Perhaps he fell in, got his feet stuck, then his thighs, found that wriggling only made matters worse. Perhaps he stood there in the bog for weeks, contemplating his death. I heard a story once of a husband and wife hopelessly lost in a cave. After days had passed and they had given up hope of rescue, they began to confide in each other as they had never done. They revealed extramarital affairs, the disdain each felt for the other's naiveté, impatience with the way one left tea bags on the counter, how the other liked the left foot to stick out of the covers at night. On and on they went, unwrapping secrets, lifting layers off their life together, until they lay weak and spent on the damp cave floor in an intimacy they had never known. Of course they were rescued. Hauled out of the labyrinth and returned to their kitchen, where they could no longer stand the sight of each other. Knowing more than they could bear, they divorced, went their separate ways. Perhaps the priest feared what the bog man had learned during his weeks of dying and didn't want such knowledge in the ground outside his church.

There are other risks with bog burials, notably that chances are you won't be found. Most of the 150 or so bog bodies we know of were discovered by peat-cutters who just happened to look down in time to see a foot or a head moments before their spades and machines cut into soft ground. Imagine how many more didn't look down. There must be thousands of bodies entombed in peat across England that have never been unearthed. And never will, now that the peat-cutting machines have passed over, now that the peat has been bagged and sold and spread over the roots of those luxuriant English gardens.

When Tollund man was unearthed in Jutland in 1950, one of the men lifting the body and knocking off chunks of surrounding peat looked at the well-preserved face, had a heart attack, and died. Tollund man's chin is stubbled with whiskers, his eyes closed, lips pressed gently together in an almost tranquil expression. He lived more than two thousand years ago, but in the photographs he looks like any number of men I know after a week of camping. His final meal of willow herb seeds, black bindwood, and mustard was still evident. Surely the past lumbers just behind us, or just below. What separates us from the dead and dying can be measured in the seconds it takes to drop through a skim of algae. Below us, the swamp gurgles, rolls over, the bog sways, its bulges and sighs visible from the boardwalk.

It is a truism in many religions that you must face your fear. If you go to therapists today instead of priests, they will tell you the same. Go straight to it, look it in the face. In fact, put your face right into it, the practitioners of certain Germanic tribal rites might have added. It was their custom to take a man who had been accused of cowardice to places like the Hingst Fen near Hanover and make him lie face down in waterlogged earth. They made sure he kept his gaze steady, eye to eye with the bog, by crisscrossing sticks over his body, plunging the ends deep into the mire, until he lay fastened to the bog as if by a pile of pick-up sticks. What to make of this? Was the guy supposed to learn something useful, to get up the next day and slosh back to the village, wringing bog water from his shirt, and tell the tribal elders he'd stared death in the face and was no longer afraid? Of course, they knew he would die there. The question is, did they, in the first century A.D., also know that his body might outlast civilizations, that he might in the 1900s be unearthed, carted over soggy fens, his teeth counted, his stomach carefully rinsed, his head removed and preserved in a mixture of toluene and wax? Was he supposed to teach us, staring at his actual face two thousand years later, something about courage?

What we learn from the bog burials has to do with who we have been. And still are. Not just our diets of barley and bristle grass, not just our intolerance of cowardice, adultery, the ways we punish thieves and murderers, our ancient need to make sacrifices to whatever brings the harvest. When we go to the Silkeborg Museum in Denmark and stare into the dark face of Tollund Man, the bog becomes an antechamber and the door is still open. What goes there in its dying might float back into the present, its face tanned and almost smiling. We may be used to the presence of the dead in cemeteries, in the leaf debris of forests, in the somber faces of daguerreotypes. We think they're on a one-way street headed away from us. But a bog is more like those rotaries I hate in Massachusetts, where you might circle for hours while other cars zoom into and out of your orbit, where whiskers on the face of a bog man brush by, your dead dog's face grins from its log frame in front of you, where you can imagine your own face unearthed from a peatbed a thousand years hence. What will they note? Your grin? Your diet of Big Macs and yogurt? The way your skin seems so real?

This water will eventually slip south, tumble over Muddy Creek Falls, thrash through Class V rapids of the Youghiogheny, and flow into the waters that drift by Pittsburgh's Three Rivers Stadium, into the Mississippi and the Gulf of Mexico. If, as some psychologists tell us, our memories are locked into the cells of our bodies, is it true for live water, too? Does the river in New Orleans remember days like this when a week of rain is like a coveted hall pass in high school – permission to leave the confines of its corridors and wander to the far edge of the building where seniors with more privilege or chutzpah pool into stairwells and smooch and feel each other up, the wild abandon of brushing the hairy stems of lady slippers, fringed petals of blue gentians? I have heard people say that rivers can heal memories, but can they hold them? Can this water dribbling from a slightly tilted bowl high in the Appalachians later slip under traffic backed up on the Huey Long Bridge and disappear into the endlessness of the gulf without losing the memory of bullfrogs bellowing from its seepy start? Can we slip through our lives without losing sight of our fingers plunged into this clogged sink of the earth, our own memories teeming with egg cases and larvae, blue damselflies and lady's-slippers, the smell of blueberries and decay? Here there is room for the elusive, the paradox, for what rocks and sways below the surface. Here the holes in the sieve of your mind open wider. Chunks of unrecognizable matter drift in. You notice your skin, how the pores themselves can open and close like millions of tiny fish mouths. You lean against the sloped sides of an invisible vortex and music pours down from the sky and you kneel in the wet bulging earth, algae clinging to your thighs, and pray that at least once in your life your own pores will open, that what knows no boundary between land and water will know no boundary at the edge of your body, that what lies riddled and pocked and hungry within you will fill and fill and fill.

.... *Barbara Hurd*

The Mystery of the Caves

I don't remember the name of the story,
but the hero, a boy, was lost,
wandering a labyrinth of caverns
filling stratum by stratum with water.

I was wondering what might happen:
would he float upward toward light?
Or would he somersault forever
in an underground black river?

I couldn't stop reading the book
because I had to know the answer,
because my mother was leaving again –
the lid of the trunk thrown open,

blouses torn from their hangers,
the crazy shouting among rooms.
The boy found it impossible to see
which passage led to safety.

One yellow finger of flame
wavered on his last match.
There was a blur of perfume –
mother breaking miniature bottles,

then my father gripping her,
but too tightly, by both arms.
The boy wasn't able to breathe.
I think he wanted me to help,

but I was small, and it was late.
And my mother was sobbing now,
no longer cursing her life,
repeating my father's name

among bright islands of skirts
circling the rim of the bed.
I can't recall the whole story,
what happened at the end....

Sometimes I worry that the boy
is still searching below the earth
for a thin pencil of light,
that I can almost hear him

through great volumes of water,
through centuries of stone,
crying my name among blind fish,
wanting so much to come home.

....Michael Waters

As a writer, skin has defined what I do because as soon as I open my front door and go out into the world, I'm no longer a private animal who would love to just delight in nature and notions about God and sanity. When I go out the front door, I'm received in a particular way, as a black male. Indoors, facing the blank page, before your God or muse, I'm one thing. But when I go outside — when I go outside and face the world and history, I realize I'm in something that's much bigger than I am, something theorized, to which I must be obedient and listen. And my voice has to negotiate with that wider world.

....Fred D'Aguiar

Minnow

I see myself as a minnow,
Small to the rest of the world.
I don't know what's happening,
Or what's going to happen –
But I swim with the waves,
The constant beating sound of drums.

As the sun rises,
And the waves glimmer,
I begin each day with courage,
Wandering in the depths of the ocean.
Not an agenda to follow,
Just swimming and swimming and swimming.

....Tracey Slaughter

Fitting

Bridesmaids, the five of us stand
in our slips, all ages and shapes showing,
waiting for her to drape the red silk,
let out the hips, take in
the cowl neck. The folds at the waist
will hide that tummy bulge, she whispers
from between her pins and lips.
Quietly bridled, we give ourselves
to her practiced eye, then shed the new chance
of each perfected dress.

In the closet, my wedding dress yellows.
This anniversary, one rose stood
for a dozen. Aspirin in the vase, and still
the bud stayed closed. I expected twice the life –
a week later buried it, shriveled and black,
under supper's chicken bones.

The calendar moves toward fall,
I stand in the rose-colored dress.
During the vows I hold my bouquet,
all shades of red, next to the bride's white orchids –
hand hers back after the bridegroom's kiss.
My tears don't come until you lay
your arm across me in the dark –
I'm singing and sewing my own white dress,
each day like crystal. It fits again,
and we dance, your spice-smell a meadow
with two young horses – far away.
The dress slips off, the music rises
like the smell of earth plowed for winter,
the tang of apples and sweet herbs,
the colts becoming one colt prancing.

.....*Barri Armitage*

Marie

Every now and again, as if on a whim, the federal government people would write to Marie Delaveaux Wilson in one of those white, stampless envelopes and tell her to come in to their place so they could take another look at her. They, the Social Security people, wrote to her in a foreign language that she had learned to translate over the years, and for all the years she had been receiving the letters the same man had been signing them. Once, because she had something important to tell him, Marie called the number the man always put at the top of the letters, but a woman answered Mr. Smith's telephone and told Marie he was in an all-day meeting. Another time she called and a man said Mr. Smith was on vacation. And finally one day a woman answered and told Marie that Mr. Smith was deceased. The woman told her to wait and she would get someone new to talk to her about her case, but Marie thought it bad luck to have telephoned a dead man and she hung up.

Now, years after the woman had told her Mr. Smith was no more, the letters were still being signed by John Smith. Come into our office at 21st and M streets, Northwest, the letters said in that foreign language. Come in so we can see if you are still blind in one eye, come in so we can see if you are still old and getting older. Come in so we can see if you still deserve to get Supplemental Security Income payments.

She always obeyed the letters, even if the order now came from a dead man, for she knew people who had been temporarily cut off from SSI for not showing up or even for being late. And once cut off, you had to move heaven and earth to get back on.

So on a not unpleasant day in March, she rose in the dark in the morning, even before the day had any sort of character, to give herself plenty of time to bathe, eat, lay out money for the bus, dress, listen to the spirituals on the radio. She was eighty-six years old, and had learned that life was all chaos and painful uncertainty and that the only way to get through it was to expect chaos even in the most innocent of moments. Offer a crust of bread to a sick bird and you often drew back a bloody finger.

John Smith's letter had told her to come in at eleven o'clock, his favorite time, and by nine that morning she had had her bath and had eaten. Dressed by nine thirty. The walk from Claridge Towers at 12th and M down to the bus stop at 14th and K took her about ten minutes, more or less. There was a bus at about ten thirty, her schedule told her, but she preferred the one that came a half hour earlier, lest there be trouble with the ten thirty bus. After she dressed, she sat at her dining room table and went over still again what papers and all else she needed to take. Given the nature of life – particularly the questions asked by the Social Security people – she always took more than they might ask for – her birth certificate, her husband's death certificate, doctors' letters.

One of the last things she put in her pocketbook was a seven-inch or so knife that she had, with the use of a small saw borrowed from a neighbor, serrated on both edges. The knife, she was convinced now, had saved her life about two weeks before. Before then she had often been careless about when she took the knife out with her, and she had never taken it out in daylight, but now she never left her apartment without it, even when going down the hall to the trash drop.

She had gone out to buy a simple box of oatmeal, no more, no less. It was about seven in the evening, the streets with enough commuters driving up 13th Street to make her feel safe. Several yards before she reached the store, the young man came from behind her and tried to rip off her coat pocket where he thought she kept her money, for she carried no purse or pocketbook after five o'clock. The money was in the other pocket with the knife, and his hand caught in the empty pocket long enough for her to reach around with the knife and cut his hand as it came out of her pocket.

He screamed and called her an old bitch. He took a few steps up 13th Street and stood in front of Emerson's Market, examining the hand and shaking off blood. Except for the cars passing up and down 13th Street, they were alone, and she began to pray.

"You cut me," he said, as if he had only been minding his own business when she cut him. "Just look what you done to my hand," he said and looked around as if for some witness to her crime. There was not a great amount of blood, but there was enough for her to see it dripping to the pavement. He seemed to be about twenty, no more than twenty-five, dressed the way they were all dressed nowadays, as if a blind man had matched up all their colors. It occurred to her to say that she had seven grandchildren his age, that by telling him this he would leave her alone. But the more filth he spoke, the more she wanted him only to come toward her again.

"You done crippled me, you old bitch."

"I sure did," she said, without malice, without triumph, but simply the way she would have told him the time of day had he asked and had she known. She gripped the knife tighter, and as she did, she turned her body ever so slightly so

74

that her good eye lined up with him. Her heart was making an awful racket, wanting to be away from him, wanting to be safe at home. I will not be moved, some organ in the neighborhood of the heart told the heart. "And I got plenty more where that come from."

The last words seemed to bring him down some and, still shaking the blood from his hand, he took a step or two back, which disappointed her. I will not be moved, that other organ kept telling the heart. "You just crazy, thas all," he said. "Just a crazy old hag." Then he turned and lumbered up toward Logan Circle, and several times he looked back over his shoulder as if afraid she might be following. A man came out of Emerson's, then a woman with two little boys. She wanted to grab each of them by the arm and tell them she had come close to losing her life. "I saved myself with this here thing," she would have said. She forgot about the oatmeal and took her raging heart back to the apartment. She told herself that she should, but she never washed the fellow's blood off the knife, and over the next few days it dried and then it began to flake off.

Toward ten o'clock that morning Wilamena Mason knocked and let herself in with a key Marie had given her.

"I see you all ready," Wilamena said.

"With the help of the Lord," Marie said. "Want a spot a coffee?"

"No thanks," Wilamena said, and dropped into a chair at the table. "Been drinkin so much coffee lately, I'm gonna turn into coffee. Was up all night with Calhoun."

"How he doin?"

Wilamena told her Calhoun was better that morning, his first good morning in over a week. Calhoun Lambeth was Wilamena's boyfriend, a seventy-five-year-old man she had taken up with six or so months before, not long after he moved in. He was the best-dressed old man Marie had ever known, but he had always appeared to be sickly, even while strutting about with his gold-tipped cane. And seeing that she could count his days on the fingers of her hands, Marie had avoided getting to know him. She could not understand why Wilamena, who could have had any man in Claridge Towers or any other senior citizen building for that matter, would take such a man into her bed. "True love," Wilamena had explained. "Avoid heartache," Marie had said, trying to be kind.

They left the apartment. Marie sought help from no one, lest she come to depend on a person too much. But since the encounter with the young man, Wilamena had insisted on escorting Marie. Marie, to avoid arguments, allowed Wilamena to walk with her from time to time to the bus stop, but no farther.

Nothing fit Marie's theory about life like the weather in Washington. Two days before the temperature had been in the forties, and yesterday it had dropped to the low twenties then warmed up a bit, with the afternoon bringing snow flurries. Today the weather people on the radio had said it would warm enough to wear just a sweater, but Marie was wearing her coat. And tomorrow, the weather people said, it would be in the thirties, with maybe an inch or so of snow.

Appointments near twelve o'clock were always risky, because the Social Security people often took off for lunch long before noon and returned sometime after one. And except for a few employees who seemed to work through their lunch hours, the place shut down. Marie had never been interviewed by someone willing to work through the lunch hour. Today, though the appointment was for eleven, she waited until one thirty before the woman at the front of the waiting room told her she would have to come back another day, because the woman who handled her case was not in.

"You put my name down when I came in like everything was all right," Marie said after she had been called up to the woman's desk.

"I know," the woman said, "but I thought that Mrs. Brown was in. They told me she was in. I'm sorry." The woman began writing in a logbook that rested between her telephone and a triptych of photographs. She handed Marie a slip and told her again she was sorry.

"Why you have me wait so long if she whatn't here?" She did not want to say too much, appear too upset, for the Social Security people could be unforgiving. And though she was used to waiting three and four hours, she found it especially unfair to wait when there was no one for her at all behind those panels the Social Security people used for offices. "I been here since before eleven."

"I know," the woman behind the desk said. "I know. I saw you there, ma'am, but I really didn't know Mrs. Brown wasn't here." There was a nameplate at the front of the woman's desk and it said Vernelle Wise. The name was surrounded by little hearts, the kind a child might have drawn.

Marie said nothing more and left.

The next appointment was two weeks later, eight thirty, a good hour, and the day before a letter signed by John Smith arrived to remind her. She expected to be out at least by twelve. Three times before eleven o'clock, Marie asked Vernelle Wise if the man, Mr. Green, who was handling her case, was in that day, and each time the woman assured her that he was. At twelve, Marie ate one of the two oranges and three of the five slices of cheese she had brought. At one, she asked again if Mr. Green was indeed in that day and politely reminded Vernelle Wise that she had been waiting since about eight that morning. Vernelle was just as polite and told her the wait would soon be over.

At one fifteen, Marie began to watch the clock hands creep around the dial. She had not paid much attention to the people about her, but more and more it seemed that others were being waited on who had arrived long after she had gotten there. After asking about Mr. Green at one, she had taken a seat near the front, and as more time went by, she found herself forced to listen to the conversation that Vernelle was having with the other receptionist next to her.

"I told him....I told him....I said just get your things and leave," said the other receptionist, who didn't have a nameplate.

"Did he leave?" Vernelle wanted to know.

"Oh, no," the other woman said. "Not at first. But I picked up some of his stuff, that Christian Dior jacket he worships. I picked up my cigarette lighter and that jacket, just like I was gonna do something bad to it, and he started movin then."

Vernelle began laughing. "I wish I was there to see that." She was filing her fingernails. Now and again she would look at her fingernails to inspect her work, and if it was satisfactory, she would blow on the nail and on the file. "He back?" Vernelle asked.

The other receptionist eyed her. "What you think?" and they both laughed.

Along about two o'clock Marie became hungry again, but she did not want to eat the rest of her food because she did not know how much longer she would be there. There was a soda machine in the corner, but all sodas gave her gas.

"You-know-who gonna call you again?" the other receptionist was asking Vernelle.

"I hope so," Vernelle said. "He pretty fly. Seemed decent too. It kinda put me off when he said he was a car mechanic. I kinda like kept tryin to take a peek at his fingernails and everything the whole evenin. See if they was dirty or what."

"Well, that mechanic stuff might be good when you get your car back. My cousin's boyfriend used to do that kinda work and he made good money, girl. I mean real good money."

"Hmmmm," Vernelle said. "Anyway, the kids like him, and you know how peculiar they can be."

"Tell me about it. They do the job your mother and father used to do, huh? Only on another level."

"You can say that again," Vernelle said.

Marie went to her and told her how long she had been waiting.

"Listen," Vernelle said, pointing her fingernail file at Marie. "I told you you'll be waited on as soon as possible. This is a busy day. So I think you should just go back to your seat until we call your name." The other reception-ist began to giggle.

Marie reached across the desk and slapped Vernelle Wise with all her might. Vernelle dropped the file, which made a cheap tinny sound when it hit the plastic board her chair was on. But no one heard the file because she had begun to cry right away. She looked at Marie as if, in the moment of her greatest need, Marie had denied her. "Oh, oh," Vernelle Wise said through the tears. "Oh, my dear God...."

The other receptionist, in her chair on casters, rolled over to Vernelle and put her arm around her. "Security!" the other receptionist hollered. "We need security here!"

The guard at the front door came quickly around the corner, one hand on his holstered gun and the other pointing accusatorially at the people seated in the waiting area. Marie had sat down and was looking at the two women almost sympathetically, as if a stranger had come in, hit Vernelle Wise, and fled.

"She slapped Vernelle!" the other receptionist said.

"Who did it?" the guard said, reaching for the man sitting beside Marie. But when the other receptionist said it was the old lady in the blue coat, the guard held back for the longest time, as if to grab her would be like arresting his own grandmother. He stood blinking and he would have gone on blinking had Marie not stood up.

She was too flustered to wait for the bus and so took a cab home. With both chains, she locked herself in the apartment, refusing to answer the door or the telephone the rest of the day and most of the next. But she knew that if her family or friends received no answer at the door or on the telephone, they would think something had happened to her. So the next afternoon, she began answering the phone and spoke with the chains on, telling Wilamena and others that she had a toothache.

For days and days after the incident she ate very little, asked God to forgive her. She was haunted by the way Vernelle's cheek had felt, by what it was like to invade and actually touch the flesh of another person. And when she thought too hard, she imagined that she was slicing through the woman's cheek, the way she had sliced through the young man's hand. But as time went on she began to remember the man's curses and the purplish color of Vernelle's fingernails, and all remorse would momentarily take flight. Finally, one morning nearly two weeks after she slapped the woman, she woke with a phrase she had not used or heard since her children were small: You whatn't raised that way.

It was the next morning that the thin young man in the suit knocked and asked through the door chains if he could speak with her. She thought that he was a Social Security man come to tear up her card and papers and tell her that they would send her no more checks. Even when he pulled out an identification card showing that he was a Howard University student, she did not believe.

In the end, she told him she didn't want to buy anything, not magazines, not candy, not anything.

"No, no," he said. "I just want to talk to you for a bit. About your life and everything. It's for a project for my folklore course. I'm talking to everyone in the building who'll let me. Please....I won't be a bother. Just a little bit of your time."

"I don't have anything worth talkin about," she said. "And I don't keep well these days."

"Oh, ma'am, I'm sorry. But we all got something to say. I promise I won't be a bother."

After fifteen minutes of his pleas, she opened the door to him because of his suit and his tie and his tie clip with a bird in flight, and because his long dark-brown fingers reminded her of delicate twigs. But had he turned out to be death with a gun or a knife or fingers to crush her neck, she would not have been surprised. "My name's George. George Carter. Like the president." He had the kind of voice that old people in her young days would have called womanish. "But I was born right here in D.C. Born, bred, and buttered, my mother used to say."

He stayed the rest of the day and she fixed him dinner. It scared her to be able to talk so freely with him, and at first she thought that at long last, as she had always feared, senility had taken hold of her. A few hours after he left, she looked his name up in the telephone book, and when a man who sounded like him answered, she hung up immediately. And the next day she did the same thing. He came back at least twice a week for many weeks and would set his cassette recorder on her coffee table. "He's takin down my whole life," she told Wilamena, almost the way a woman might speak in awe of a new boyfriend.

One day he played back for the first time some of what she told the recorder:

> ....*My father would be sittin there readin the paper. He'd say whenever they put in a new president, "Look like he got the chair for four years." And it got so that's what I saw — this poor man sittin in that chair for four long years while the rest of the world went on about its business. I don't know if I thought he ever did anything, the president. I just knew that he had to sit in that chair for four years. Maybe I thought that by his sittin in that chair and doin nothin else for four years he made the country what it was and that without him sittin there the country wouldn't be what it was. Maybe thas what I got from listenin to my father readin and to my mother askin him questions bout what he was readin. They was like that, you see....*

George stopped the tape and was about to put the other side in when she touched his hand.

"No more, George," she said. "I can't listen to no more. Please.... please, no more." She had never in her whole life heard her own voice. Nothing had been so stunning in a long, long while, and for a few moments before she found herself, her world turned upside down. There, rising from a machine no bigger than her Bible, was a voice frighteningly familiar and yet unfamiliar, talking about a man whom she knew as well as her husbands and her sons, a man dead and buried sixty years. She reached across to George and he handed her the tape. She turned it over and over, as if the mystery of everything could be discerned if she turned it enough times. She began to cry, and with her other hand she lightly touched the buttons of the machine.

Between the time Marie slapped the woman in the Social Security office and the day she heard her voice for the first time, Calhoun Lambeth, Wilamena's boyfriend, had been in and out the hospital three times. Most evenings when Calhoun's son stayed the night with him, Wilamena would come up to Marie's and spend most of the evening, sitting on the couch that was catty-corner to the easy chair facing the big window. She said very little, which was unlike her, a woman with more friends than hairs on her head and who, at sixty-eight, loved a good party. The most attractive woman Marie knew would only curl her legs up under herself and sip whatever Marie put in her hand. She looked out at the city until she took herself to her apartment or went back down to Calhoun's place. In the beginning, after he returned from the hospital the first time, there was the desire in Marie to remind her friend that she wasn't married to Calhoun, that she should just get up and walk away, something Marie had seen her do with other men she had grown tired of.

Late one night, Wilamena called and asked her to come down to the man's apartment, for the man's son had had to work that night and she was there alone with him and she did not want to be alone with him. "Sit with me a spell," Wilamena said. Marie did not protest, even though she had not said more than ten words to the man in all the time she knew him. She threw on her bathrobe, picked up her keys and serrated knife, and went down to the second floor.

He was propped up on the bed, and he was surprisingly alert and spoke to Marie with an unforced friendliness. She had seen this in other dying people – a kindness and gentleness came over them that was often embarrassing for those around them. Wilamena sat on the side of the bed. Calhoun asked Marie to sit in a chair beside the bed and then he took her hand and held it for the rest of the night. He talked on throughout the night, not always understandable. Wilamena, exhausted, eventually lay across the foot of the bed. Almost everything the man had to say was about a time when he was young and was married for a year or so to a woman in Nicodemus, Kansas, a town where there were only black people. Whether the woman had died or whether he had left her, Marie could not make out. She only knew that the woman and Nicodemus seemed to have marked him for life.

"You should go to Nicodemus," he said at one point, as if the town was only around the corner. "I stumbled into the place by accident. But you should go on purpose. There ain't much to see, but you should go there and spend some time there."

Toward four o'clock that morning, he stopped talking and moments later he went home to his God. Marie continued holding the dead man's hand and she said the Lord's prayer over and over until it no longer made sense to her. She did not wake Wilamena. Eventually, the sun came through the man's venetian blinds and she heard the croaking of the pigeons congregating on the window ledge. When she finally placed his hand on his chest, the dead man expelled a burst of air that sounded to Marie like a sigh. It occurred to her that she, a complete stranger, was the last thing he had known in the world and that now that he was no longer in the world all she knew of him was that Nicodemus place and a lovesick woman asleep at the foot of his bed. She thought that she was hungry and thirsty, but the more she looked at the dead man and the sleeping woman, the more she realized that what she felt was a sense of loss.

Two days later, the Social Security people sent her a letter, again signed by John Smith, telling her to come to them one week hence. There was nothing in the letter about the slap, no threat to cut off her SSI payments because of what she had done. Indeed, it was the same sort of letter John Smith usually sent. She called the number at the top of the letter, and the woman who handled her case told her that Mrs. White would be expecting her on the day and time stated in the letter. Still, she suspected the Social Security people were planning something for her, something at the very least that would be humiliating. And, right up until the day before the appointment, she continued calling to confirm that it was okay to come in. Often, the person she spoke to after the switch-board woman and before the woman handling her case was Vernelle. "Social Security Administration. This is Vernelle Wise. May I help you?" And each time Marie heard the receptionist identify herself she wanted to apologize. "I whatn't raised that way," she wanted to tell the woman.

George Carter came the day she got the letter to present her with a cassette machine and copies of the tapes she had made about her life. It took quite some time for him to teach her how to use the machine, and after he was gone, she was certain it took so long because she really did not want to know how to use it. That evening, after her dinner, she steeled herself and put a tape marked "Parents; Early Childhood" in the machine.

> ....*My mother had this idea that everything could be done in Washington, that a human bein could take all they troubles to Washington and things would be set right. I think that was all wrapped up with her notion of the govment, the Supreme Court and the president and the like. "Up there," she would say, "things can be made right." "Up there" was her only words for Washington. All them other cities had names, but Washington didn't need a name. It was just called "up there." I was real small and didn't know any better, so somehow I got to thinkin since things were on the perfect side in Washington, that maybe God lived there. God and his people....When I went back home to visit that first time and told my mother all about my livin in Washington, she fell into such a cry, like maybe I had managed to make it to heaven without dyin. Thas how people was back in those days....*

The next morning she looked for Vernelle Wise's name in the telephone book. And for several evenings she would call the number and hang up before the phone had rung three times. Finally, on a Sunday, two days before the appointment, she let it ring and what may have been a little boy answered. She could tell he was very young because he said "Hello" in a too-loud voice, as if he was not used to talking on the telephone.

"Hello," he said. "Hello, who this? Granddaddy, that you? Hello. Hello. I can see you."

Marie heard Vernelle tell him to put down the telephone, then another child, perhaps a girl somewhat older than the boy, came on the line. "Hello. Hello. Who is this?" she said with authority. The boy began to cry, apparently because he did not want the girl to talk if he couldn't. "Don't touch it," the girl said. "Leave it alone." The boy cried louder and only stopped when Vernelle came to the telephone.

"Yes?" Vernelle said. "Yes." Then she went off the line to calm the boy who had again begun to cry. "Loretta," she said, "go get his bottle....Well, look for it. What you got eyes for?"

There seemed to be a second boy, because Vernelle told him to help Loretta look for the bottle. "He always losin things," Marie heard the second boy say. "You should tie everything to his arms." "Don't tell me what to do," Vernelle said. "Just look for that damn bottle."

"I don't lose nofin. I don't," the first boy said. "You got snot in your nose."

"Don't say that," Vernelle said before she came back on the line. "I'm sorry," she said to Marie. "Who is this? ....Don't you dare touch it if you know what's good for you!" she said. "I wanna talk to Granddaddy," the first boy said. "Loretta, get me that bottle!"

Marie hung up. She washed her dinner dishes. She called Wilamena because she had not seen her all day, and Wilamena told her that she would be up later. The cassette tapes were on the coffee table beside the machine, and she began picking them up, one by one. She read the labels. "Husband No. 1." "Working." "Husband No. 2." "Children." "Race Relations." "Early D.C. Experiences." "Husband No. 3." She had not played another tape since the one about her mother's idea of what Washington was like, but she could still hear the voice, her voice. Without reading its label, she put a tape in the machine.

> ....I never planned to live in Washington, had no idea I would ever even step one foot in this city. This white family my mother worked for, they had a son married and gone to live in Baltimore. He wanted a maid, somebody to take care of his children. So he wrote to his mother and she asked my mother and my mother asked me about goin to live in Baltimore. Well, I was young. I guess I wanted to see the world, and Baltimore was as good a place to start as anywhere. This man sent me a train ticket and I went off to Baltimore. Hadn't ever been kissed, hadn't ever been anything, but here I was goin farther from home than my mother and father put together.... Well, sir, the train stopped in Washington, and I thought I

heard the conductor say we would be stoppin a bit there, so I got off. I knew I probably wouldn't see no more than that Union Station, but I wanted to be able to say I'd done that, that I step foot in the capital of the United States. I walked down to the end of the platform and looked around, then I peeked into the station. Then I went in. And when I got back, the train and my suitcase was gone. Everything I had in the world on the way to Baltimore....

....I couldn't calm myself anough to listen to when the redcap said another train would be leavin for Baltimore, I was just that upset. I had a buncha addresses of people we knew all the way from home up to Boston, and I used one precious nickel to call a woman I hadn't seen in years, cause I didn't have the white people in Baltimore number. This woman come and got me, took me to her place. I member like it was yesterday, that we got on this streetcar marked 13th and D NE. The more I rode, the more brighter things got. You ain't lived till you been on a streetcar. The further we went on that streetcar – dead down in the middle of the street – the more I knowed I could never go live in Baltimore. I knowed I could never live in a place that didn't have that streetcar and them clackety-clack tracks....

She wrapped the tapes in two plastic bags and put them in the dresser drawer that contained all that was valuable to her – birth and death certificates, silver dollars, life insurance policies, pictures of her husbands and the children they had given each other, and the grandchildren those children had given her and the great-grands whose names she had trouble remembering. She set the tapes in a back corner of the drawer, away from the things she needed to get her hands on regularly. She knew that however long she lived, she would not ever again listen to them, for in the end, despite all that was on the tapes, she could not stand the sound of her own voice.

....Edward P. Jones

A Fortunate Catch

The gill looks like a wound,
doesn't it? Hooked by the scythe
of a crescent moon that held him
dangling, he dropped here, raw.

A mouth looks like that
in a candid shot, caught
at a barbecue, as the jaws
fall open in surprise.

Twisting and trying to swim
in sand now, the bluefish
for all the show is helpless.
Here, at shore's edge,

the sea washes up foam,
10 a.m., paying back the moon
her low interest loan.
The fish's old sunken eye

never closes. Shaped like a tear,
the fish is trying to pull
away from itself. Again the tail
lifts into the air, reaches

for small planets, lost home seas.
Now it raises its thin red veils,
begins to move seaward. Take note,
you flies and dragonflies,

you sandpipers and starfish.
Here comes a little life!
Sing out, call for it. Did I mention
how the fin resembles a wing?

...Jacklyn W. Potter

The Forgotten American

not to consider this
forgotten man
is to miss
America

you must record the facts: he

comes home dog-tired
    guzzles beer in his T-shirt,
watches the ball game intensely,
    spots flaws in the play.

he
    carves at table,
eats solemnly,
    chews and swallows,
wipes his lips,
    sips his drink,
gets up without excuses

is baffled by the news,
    talks to the tv,
vows trouble for the troublemakers,
    doesn't always approve of
the President

falls asleep on the couch,
    wakes up groggy,
climbs the stairs unsteadily,
    showers, brushes,
feels good in freshly-washed pajamas,
    loves his sleep.

he
    wakes early,
pisses, shakes dry, zips up,
    splashes cold water on his face,

frowns in the mirror,
    combs his hair,
pours sugar in his coffee,
    reads the paper hastily,
pecks the wife at the door

drives to work in a daze,
    is weak at red lights,
strong on the freeway,
    works from strange necessity,
breaks for coffee,
    munches his lunch-time sandwich distractedly,
watches the clock.

he
    pays his bills,
sometimes gets a raise,
    is regular with his wife,
threatens the kids,
    scratches where it itches

knows when he's hungry,
    makes predictions,
sweats as he mows, rakes, or shovels,
    strains for his stool,
balances his budget,
    feels as good as his money.

consider this man
who signs his name, waves, likes
the sun;
consider him
and reach out your hand:
    he will shake it
    instinctively.

....William Heath

Still Life
in chalk on asphalt

Muggy August is in the house,
the thick air sticking a shirt
into the curve of your back.
You go out for a banana Slurpee,
close the door like the cover of a book,
tilt your head and hope for rain.
The stars stand out like grains of salt
spilled across a black tablecloth.
You hang a right on the Ave,
pass the Liquor store's grinning Colt .45 sign.
The moon shines like a cue ball about to break up
the hustlers clustered on the corner.
Jeans hang loose on their hips,
their noses sniff for the smell of green.
You shake your head to the question
yellowing in their eyes.
A Jeep booms by, trailing a ribbon of rapping,
its tires whispering circular secrets
into the asphalt's ear.
Around the corner where the 7-11 sits,
the rotating arm atop an ambulance
slaps two paramedics crouched
over a young boy in the street.
His eyes and mouth are drawn open,
the thought balloon above him, empty.
Cherry Kool-Aid stains his shirt,
his sneakers are white as a kilo of coke.
All the trees have their arms in the air.
The witness' fingers disagree
on the number of shots.
His mother collapses against a mailbox,
weary lines penciled on her face,
dark blues bleeding down the back of her throat.
Her cheeks shiny under watercolored eyes,

fingers soaked with a fleeting soul,
she cradles his cooling body,
his name sits crooked on her lips.
The parked cars stare silently ahead
as the sound of red begins to reign.

....dj renegade

Elegy for the Other Woman

May her plane explode
with just one fatality.
But, should it not,
may the other woman spew
persistent dysentery
from your first night ever after.
May the other woman vomit
African bees and Argentine wasps.
May cobras uncoil from her loins.
May she be eaten not
by something dramatic like lions,
but by a wart-hog.
I do not wish the other woman
to fall down a well
for fear of spoiling the water,
nor die on the highway because
she might obstruct traffic.
Rather: something easy, and cheap,
like clap from some other bloke.
Should she nevertheless survive
all these critical possibilities,
may she quietly die of boredom with you.

.... Elisavietta Ritchie

Trying Out a Blazer 4-By

A hundred and sixty five horses over
a truck chassis – it rides high and the view
opens beyond car-lot fence to fields,
to hills. On the road I'm level with an Exxon tanker,
as we pass the driver lifts a thumb in greeting.

I am unused to the quick response, the surge
uphill, I've settled for what's adequate,
but the sly taste of power meagers that, an appetite
wakes for steeper slopes, rougher tracks.

A bicyclist yaws against the grade, his dog
loping beside him, I gun the motor and they're
a blip in the rearview mirror. Enhanced
by a V-8 engine and the arrogance it bestows,
a hidden penchant to belittle outs, with a rush
of scorn I pull past a white sedan,
the woman driving, gray-haired as I.

Wait, hold on. This is how wars begin.

I downshift and swerve onto a lumber road,
shocks take the washboard bumps, wheels
crush a burst of Christmas fern but a fallen
pine tree blocks my way. I stop, kill
the motor and sudden silence clamps in.

Then rustle, tick, the sharp slice of a jay's
call and a drift of something heady, sweet
I cannot name. Just as well this halt
to turbulence that skewed me from a well-mapped
path. It's not the loosing of horses I fear,
but the unbridled wilderness opened in my belly.

....Ann B. Knox

The music was jammin
She came to dance
She didn't wait for anyone to ask for permission
She didn't sit alone on a stool inside herself
Smoking a cigarette
She shook her high step karate kick
Soft clenched fist rippling body back and forth
Across the barren dance floor
A visual stream of sensual consciousness
In a startled sea
I danced with her once before they threw
Her out

Her name was Debbie
She worked in a bar in the suburbs
She didn't get out much
Her husband was a drunk who slept around
And didn't appreciate her
But she loved him and was faithful anyway
She ran hot and cold and even spoke of God
Between tongue kisses
We laughed like two forgetful lovers
Forgetting for a moment how alone we really were
Gently holding my arm, she rested her head
On my shoulder
We kissed goodbye
I took her home to him

....Terry Edmonds

Christmas Eve: My Mother Dressing

My mother was not impressed with her beauty;
once a year she put it on like a costume,
plaited her black hair, slick as cornsilk, down past her hips,
in one rope-thick braid, turned it, carefully, hand over hand,
and fixed it at the nape of her neck, stiff and elegant as a crown,
with tortoise pins, like huge insects,
some belonging to her dead mother,
some to my living grandmother.
Sitting on the stool at the mirror,
she applied a peachy foundation that seemed to hold her down,
     to trap her,
as if we never would have noticed what flew among us unless
     it was weighted and bound in its mask.
Vaseline shined her eyebrows,
mascara blackened her lashes until they swept down like feathers;
her eyes deepened until they shone from far away.

Now I remember her hands, her poor hands, which, even then
     were old from scrubbing,
whiter on the inside than they should have been,
and hard, the first joints of her fingers, little fattened pads,
the nails filed to sharp points like old-fashioned ink pens,
     painted a jolly color.
Her hands stood next to her face and wanted to be put away,
     prayed
for the scrub bucket and brush to make them useful.
And, as I write, I forget the years I watched her
pull hairs like a witch from her chin, magnify
every blotch – as if acid were thrown from the inside.

But once a year my mother
rose in her white silk slip,
not the slave of the house, the woman,
took the ironed dress from the hanger –
allowing me to stand on the bed, so that
my face looked directly into her face,
and hold the garment away from her
as she pulled it down.

....*Toi Derricotte*

August

The only odalisque I know is August
whose hours open like a kiss
that lasts all afternoon. Notice how
she dips her slender fingers into the cool
mint tea of evening, languidly wrapping
her turban as if to protect her head,
from that clear-eyed and ambitious Fall.
She knows her days are waning,
that soon enough she'll be packed
for storage like a mistress or a vase
emptied of stems, of summer, of an ocean
too cold now for swimming. But she's
in no hurry. Her limbs are tanned
curving along the chaise longue.
That over-the-shoulder half-smile
she gives you still mysteriously beckons.
If she invites you to recline with her, do.

....*Christina Daub*

Barbara Fritchie, Departing

Most mornings one or more of us is elbowed
out of upstairs windows here in Frederick,
keeping a check on the cities marching
in on either flank. The investors say
it's about as inevitable as rain.
We say as welcome as taxes, death.

Afternoons, we're packing up. We post
a woman on a roof in town, measure
the sight lines up the valleys
toward Washington and Baltimore,
tell her to sing out when she sees
the graders, bulldozers and cranes

come down those final grades toward us.
The modest shadows that our buildings throw
across the shoulders of low roof and gable
are quiet clocks that measure quiet days.
We plan to take the shadows along
when we go. The city folk have their own

to truck across the mountain. We'll leave
at night, steal out when the signal's given.
Nothing of us, not even a line, will remain
except a painting of the door we've closed.
For safety's sake, the artist has removed
the handle from the door, left no address.

....Martin Galvin

February 27, 1999

Sleeping into my sixty-fifth birthday,
what obsesses me, what I dream and
brood about and chew on, each time
my prostate rouses me – which is often –
is not my surprising age or unsurprising
prostate but an item in the news about
the news:

      that ABC will air – for 120
minutes – Barbara Walters' 80-minute
interview with Monica Lewinsky,
the discrepant forty minutes given to
commercials so expensive the network's
take is thirty to thirty-five million.

Meanwhile ABC gloats about not paying
Monica, when British tellie did, as if
it's a matter of American journalistic
principle, this bottom-line hypocrisy.

Why *not* pay Monica – and Bill too, his
and Hilary's nine million (and counting)
legal fees? If paying nothing, ABC should
make nothing – and show it commercial-free.

Instead it charges corporate America, and
all of us for what we've already paid for,
in spades, for two years, like alimony,
the screwing you get for the screwing
you got (though here, maybe, no one did).

So – will I boycott it as I should? Maybe.
Maybe not. Berryman said of his obnoxious
absorption in *Time* that he despised it
cover to cover once a week. And so may I
annoy myself, start to finish, with this
Barbara-Monica smarm-fest. But maybe not.

For now, still grumpy,
I wish myself a happy sixty-fifth –
pen in hand, at least, pen in hand.

.....*Roland Flint*

*Good writing invites us, as writers and readers, to immerse
ourselves in a very particular landscape, an immersion which helps
us open to new and richer ways of seeing ourselves and our
surroundings. I think of these immersions as opportunities 1) to
move from the abstraction to the particular; 2) to reconsider our
notion of beauty; 3) to read and write without cynical detachment
or heart-bleeding sentimentality, but in full acknowledgement of the
cycles of birth and death and rebirth; 4) to associate, at least once
in a while, with histories that are not "made in our image"; 5) to
realize that our spiritual and imaginative selves might be at least
partly shaped by something other than we thought.*

.....*Barbara Hurd*

We can't heal the world until we can heal ourselves.

.....*Grace Cavalieri*

Grief

You drive home, a bobber
in your throat tugging. You tell your wife
you're all right, then squeeze tight the bedroom door.
You empty the change from your pocket.
The bobber tugging, you lie
on your side of the bed
and, in the dark there, pull up your grief
like a thirty pound muskie.

With your teeth you cut the line; the fish
swims through the bedroom air,
its dorsal fin gliding
across the ceiling, its scales
grazing your face.
The air is water here.

Your wife comes in.
The kids can hear you,
she says, *they're scared.*
She throws open a window, enough
for the grief to slip through.
She sits on the side of the bed and holds you
the way your mother did. She tells you dinner is ready.

Scales glitter on the dark sill.

....William Palmer

Fires at Yellowstone

My mother calls today
with news of the Pennsylvania sun
burnt the color of candied oranges,

of noon turned dusk by faraway
disaster. How can it be?
Then Jack reminds me

of Mount St. Helens' ash
that darkened the sky it fell
through, of rice fields smoldering

in the California of his youth, the ash
settling on the hopscotch of Sacramento's
rooftops and lawns.
The current misplaced darkness

is from well-traveled smoke
that once was trees,
thousands and thousands of acres of trees
left to burn naturally too long.

When I was nine, I stood beside Old Faithful.
Snapshots confirm
that in my green Nehru jacket
I bounded from the '63 Ford wagon;

and in the dream beyond the photo,
the geyser reached up toward the Tetons or Sierras,
drifting mist across the wheat fields of Kansas,

across Indiana smokestacks and the long pull
of Ohio, before settling on a small town
in the Alleghenies, which was home.

The day my son was born
every tree in my body was razed,
and this great pain burnt thousands of acres
of everything I thought I could be.

It's October,
and our own paling Maryland sun leaves
a little earlier now;
my son asks where it goes.

And when I tell him how far
Earth must turn,
I think of Yellowstone,

I think of saplings sprouting from the body
that has been so blackened and enriched by disaster.

...Julia Wendell

For Chris

to you who said your father threw you
through the living room window who showed me
the scars from your neck to your navel
where the doctors cut open to fix
the eleven-year-old valves of your heart
there are things we hear with our calcareous hearts
that will drive us from the sanctified natures of our rooms
into the cold vast skies of a moonless night
where each star with its own blinking language
reveals unreachable solitude to us
I walked my angers till I ran out of streets
and barking dogs remembering the hours I spent
as a child listening to the sound of love
weeping through the walls of our house
from the welts of our father's embraces
the only ones he ever knew what can I tell you
but that love is an inparticular compass
that there is only one true angel
and her name is Innocence and the only choice
children have is to make laughter and play
out of melancholy I walked past the last street lamp
and stood in the shivering loneliness
of a dark road that led to some forever
I could no longer see though I was aware
of my blindness and of the impalpable sounds
of struggling gasps I have heard
coming from my own son when he is unable to catch
a single breath as he tries to muffle
the anguished and flailing love of his father
life is truly the most beautiful tragedy
I thought finding no wisdom or comfort in that
I turned back and as I turned I heard the lament
of a siren and the mongrels who quickly joined in

that harmony of sorrows piercing the darkness
erasing my footfalls and as I walked away I turned
to search that unplaceable howl and saw an explosion
of moonlight rising along the arc
of a perfect evening and I remembered what we see
and hear is only half of a story
you who stirred my silent dominions
who startled the fallen forms of purity introducing me
to all your fifth grade friends and who said
the thing you liked best is to go fishing
whenever your father comes to visit you thank you
thank you for guiding me back to my faith
in the powers of mystery

....*Edgar Silex*

Instructions for Dying

When they call you from the grave, you must
Swim upward, using a winding stroke.
You must ascend swiftly through dark green
Pressures, before your eardrums burst with the force
Of what is spinning by. If you black out,
Consciousness will return, though spiral swimming
Dizzies the identity. Rise
Toward light with lungs strained to endure
The cries of drowning voices, sirens who pluck
The swimmers from the lonely vortex. Rise
Through shimmering green, past moments of forgetting
Till almost at the surface, one
Last leap toward light, then the final
Layer of foam – and burst out into air,
A child with no name, breathing above
The waters, who never learned to swim.

.....*Larry Rubin*

Don't Postpone Joy

a butterfly
minus
cell phone,
contacts,
or resume,

skitters
along the
somber buildings
of farragut square.

does not crowd
into the ubiquitous
buffet by the
pound
delicatessens
that will close

like broken wings
at rush hour,

choosing instead
to be guided by /

to dine on the wind

we promise ourselves
we too will kiss

when we retire

....reuben jackson

Bedtime Story

Something small and dark lay crouched
at the back of my throat
waiting its slow souring wait
until it would wait no longer.

The boy was already cowering;
the words he'd said had dropped
like a heavy, poisonous dram
swirling the waters of our anxious love.

Who can tell why this needed
to be said, or why the closed bolt
of my rage could not hold tight against it?

It was the same old thing,
me calling him out for the forming man
in him filling the child's mouth with words.

Don't talk back to your father, I said.

But the spell would not be cast this time.
That man possessed the quavering child
and only the pale child's shell
stood before me. A voice like my own
unleashed a black hail against the trigger
of my resolve.

And that dark thing
knew that its time had come again,
wheeled on fierce wings and grew
immense as the winter night.

I'd had to let go to gain myself back,
but the boy had no defense against it:
he could neither run nor strike it down,
only let it do its horror and spend itself
as all the demons finally do that spring from us,
unwanted, changing the colors of our hearts.

....*Phillip K. Jason*

Returning to the City By Boat

A young girl stiffens her arm
in the shrill of a whistle.
Her cheeks harden and she points ashore
to a square light in a far building
echoing 'home, home'
as if she'd come home
from school this way for years,
shuffling these lights
like stones along the street.

And facing these lights, trembling
as the boat drifts
near, I watch this girl beside me
fingering the hem of her lace
dress, holding it to her knees,
keeping warm. And hear mother
in the next room stitching
clothes at night, waves
of cloth piling onto the floor,
darker as the hems grow deep.

And I remember as the bay
strays into harbor and twelve
herons watch the city dredge
stars from the night,
that we have no home but space
between two hems.

The girl lowers her thin arm,
wind falls into a pleat
of waves, my dress curls around
my white knees, as the young girl
clutches the iron railing and leans
over, far down, home into the streets.

....Kathy Wagner

He knew the wounded old chair was in pain yet Dr. Z. could not bring himself to put it out of its misery. The eczema-like rash on its once shiny leatherette arms, the scars and pits created by the dug-in nails of generations of patients, the yellowed guts that poked through the tufted seat cushion, especially where its buttons had been torn loose: he knew the chair was suffering but still chose to keep it alive so after the last patient of the day left he could turn to it, at first to stare in wonder, then gently to ask questions. What dreams, what anguished secrets, what litanies of recollected childhood insults had been absorbed by this chair! What deep impressions had been left in its flesh!

Whom else could he ask, probing gently of course, the name of that stunning woman from the early days of his practice, the woman who had peeled off a strip of the chair's skin when telling the story of her rapacious uncles, a story so terrible it had made a lasting imprint on both his head and heart. What had happened to her, he wondered. Had his carefully chosen words helped her to live a satisfying life after she freed herself from his care, or was she still cowering somewhere in misery, her face beaten, her once lovely hair hanging in shanks? Only the chair could provide an answer and often it was reluctant to do so – not because of any moral compunctions but because given the great number of patients who had sat in its lap facing him as he listened intently from his own chair, his feet resting on its hassock so his patients could focus on the soles of his shoes if they wished to avoid his eyes, the chair sometimes became confused.

But even if the chair could not answer, he continued to ask questions. The bearded man who threatened to kill the small boy his wife refused to let him see, the man he had to eject from his office under police guard: was he behind bars or cheerfully tossing a frisbee to one of the neighborhood kids? The plump woman who thought no one in the world loved her, twisting one of the chair's buttons as she haltingly spoke: had she at last found happiness?

And so it went on, though his present patients never ceased to complain when the chair's exposed nails or rough skin tore their sleeves, when the seat of their pants got stuck in one of the chair's great canyons. One woman even threatened to peel off what remained of the leatherette skin, thus exposing everything the chair contained, never mind previous patients' rights to privacy. Went on until one day the chair slumped over onto the worn oriental rug carrying Dr. Z. with it – though by the time the custodian came to clean the office that night it was impossible to tell that the doctor himself had actually been sitting in the chair at its penultimate moment. So many colleagues and former patients attended the chair's funeral that they spilled out onto the street in front of the chapel. Dr. Z. managed to get through the rites with dry eyes, but soon afterwards, having with much anguish replaced the late chair with the closest replication he could find, he decided to give up his practice.

His own young replacement ordered a jaunty modern chair from Finland, its frame painted with so many layers of bright yellow lacquer its back and arms could not absorb a single secret. And no matter how hard people tried, they could not leave so much as a scratch, at best a fingerprint the young replacement would quickly rub off with one deft stroke of a kleenex. Soon nobody even wanted to leave a mark. None remembered a dream or a catastrophic childhood moment. And certainly not a single patient stayed in treatment long enough to make an impression of any sort – assuming it was even remotely possible to impress steel.

....Barbara F. Lefcowitz

Afterwards, You Learn

Afterwards, you learn to say
you were lucky, the last-year's cubs
stayed safely behind her, breaking
the thickets for berries. Lucky
the wind from the darkening valley
turned cold, and your jacket was heavy,
and zipped to the neck. Lucky
you knew, too late for retreat
in that clearing of downfall and stone,
to drop and go fetal, arm
over neck, playing dead. Lucky
the backpack came off like an arm,
saving most of your arm, and kept her
busy till the grunting cubs
called her back to their feast.

Afterwards you learn to say
that the fault was yours: you were tired,
you were stubborn, making up for lost time
on that summer-growth trail through clearings
and thickets, the wind in your face,
not bothering to sing out or warn
what was there besides you, not waiting
for warnings to reach you.

But sometimes, in sleep, you go back
to that stonefall clearing, that edge
of safety where your scalp hair rises
like hackles for no reason you see,
and there is still enough time to go back
as that dark shape lifts upright
from its tangle of shadow, like a man
in a burly fur suit, peering out,
and you wake with the ghost hairs rising
like fur on your unscarred neck
and perfect right arm.

                              ...Judith McCombs

Depression

You start out with a tree in the ground
You get shade and fruit and color
And it's great

Then they take away the ground, leaving you the tree
And though the tree is dying
You still get shade and color
You remember the fruit
And it's okay

Then they take away the tree, leaving you
   a leaf
And though you've lost a lot
You still get the color
You remember the shade
But you forget about the fruit
And it's ...fine

Then they take away the leaf, leaving you a stem
And though it's not much by itself
You can remember the color
But you forget about the shade
And the fruit is long gone
And it's bad

Then they take away the stem, leaving you with
   nothing
And now there's nothing there
You've forgotten all the colors
The shade has long since passed
And you don't even know what fruit is, now
And the clinical name
Is depression

....Ben Moldover

At the Library

See the young girl
beside the window
bending over a book,
her dark hair shines
with floating dust fired
by sun tilting through glass.
See how she lifts her face
to the wall, seeing nothing,
seeing everything.
She is not here,
yet she is here.
I see her motionless,
tense but perfectly still.
She rides the invisible
flow of inspiration,
on a stream of language,
probes her own ideas
fused with vast musings
from the book she holds
open with slim fingers.
She fashions her own visions
guarded by a mysterious smile,
suspends the moment – a flash
where life gushes and flows
in a fountain of light.
My heart tells me
the young gather food
for the mind as naturally
as sparrows hunger for ripe
seeds sorted from grass.

....Stacy E. Tuthill

Passage of a Hunter

for Alden Capen

Now unseen, you stalk
invisible deer in the forest.
Wind gusts suddenly.
Crows lift ahead of you
in a clamor of fright as
dead leaves blow like
spume in your wake.

And I am frightened.
You are becoming something
random, unknown, the green
man melting into oak
wild as what you hunt.

.....Kathy Pearce-Lewis

If we don't tell our stories, we are in danger of allowing others to make up our stories for us. The writer has to be willing to risk going to that place where all loss and anger and love and sorrow and joy hide. We have to give ourselves permission to speak and write the truth.

....Maria Mazziotti Gillan

Proof

Today the maples become
suddenly generous, showering
their webbed pods everywhere.
The screens go up. Front to back,
wind blows through the house.
Neighbors appear in their yards:
two women rasp at each other
over a fence, as if rediscovering
their voices. Dogs bark back
and forth in shade. The postman
comes by on foot, drops
a letter in my box.
            Three days ago,
a friend was thinking of me.
What more proof do I need?
Out on the river, the last splinter
of ice returns to the river.

.....*Kathy Mangan*

Dragon's Seed

for Catherine Mims

Mackie Loudon lived alone in a small house made of iron and stone on a short street west of Twenty-first Avenue. She had lived there, alone, for a long time. Old ivy grew in a carpet across her front steps and in her yard the grass was tall, with volunteer shoots of privet standing in it. The street was old enough to have a few big trees and the houses were raised on a high embankment above the sidewalk. It was quiet down the whole length of her block, almost always very, very quiet.

Indoors, it seemed that inertia ruled, though maybe that was just a first impression. The front room had once been a parlor, but now, scattered among the original furnishings were all of Mackie Loudon's sculpture tools. There were pole lamps, a rocker, a couple of armchairs, some fragile little end tables, also hammers and chisels and files and other devices, and a variety of sculptures in wood and stone. In former times people had come from the North to take the sculptures away and sell them, but it was a long time since their visits had stopped. She did not remember the reason or care about it, since she was not in want.

The things she didn't need to use stayed put exactly where they were. In the kitchen, on the gas stove, an iron skillet sat with browning shreds of egg still plastered to it, a relic of the very last time Mackie Loudon had bothered to make herself a hot meal. Asians had moved to a storefront within walking distance of her house, to open a store and cafeteria, and she went there to provender herself with things she never knew the names of. She bought salt plums, and packets of tiny dried fish whose eyes were bigger than their heads, and crocks of buried vegetables plugged with mud. She dumped the empty containers in the sink, and when it filled she bagged them up and carried the bag down a rickety outside staircase to a place in the alley from where it would eventually disappear. There was one pot that she used for coffee and that was all. On the window sill above the sink was an old teacup, its inside covered with a filigree of tiny tannin-colored cracks. Each morning, if the day was fair, a bar of sunlight would find a painted rose on its upper rim, warm it a moment, then pass on.

She wore flowered cotton dresses, knee length with no shape, and in winter a man's tweed overcoat. With the light behind her, her legs showed through the fabric. They were very slightly bowed, and her shoulders were rather big for a woman, her hands strong. She had a little trouble with arthritis, but not so much she couldn't work. Her features were flat, her skin strong and wrinkly like elephant hide. A few long white hairs flew away from her chin. The rest of her hair was thick and gray, and she hacked it off herself in a rough helmet shape and peered out from underneath its visor. Her right eye was green, her left pale blue and troubled by an unusual sort of tic. Over five or so minutes the eyelid would lower, imperceptibly and inexorably closing itself till it was fully shut, and then quite suddenly fly back open in a startled blue awakening. Because of this, some said that Mackie Loudon had the evil eye, and others thought she was a witch, which was not true, although she did hold colloquy with demons.

Before the fireplace in the parlor was a five-foot length of a big walnut log, out of which Mackie Loudon was carving a great head of Medusa. For a workstand she used a stone sculpture she'd forgotten, mostly a flat-topped limestone rock with an ill-defined head and arm of Sisyphus just visible underneath it. She stood on a rotting embroidered ottoman to reach the top of the section of wood, and took her chisels from the mantelpiece where they were lined. The front windows had not been washed in years and what light came through was weak and dingy, but she could see as much as she required to. Her chisels were ordered from New York and each was sharp enough to shave with. She didn't often need to use her mallets; wherever she touched her scoop to its surface the walnut curled away like butter. She carved, the strange eye opened and closed on its offbeat rhythm and the murmur and mutter of her demons soothed her like a song.

There were two of them, Eliel and Azazael. Each made occasional inconsistent protestations of being good, or evil. Often they quarreled, with each other or with her, and at other times they would cooperate in the interlocking way of opposites. Eliel reported himself to be the spirit of air and Azazael the spirit of darkness. Sometimes they would exchange these roles, or sometimes both would compete to occupy one or the other. They laid conflicting claims to powers of memory and magic, though Mackie Loudon could always point out that there was little enough in the real world they'd ever accomplished on their own.

Azazael was usually hostile to Medusa. *You don't know what you're getting into,* he said. *You're not sure yourself just what you're calling up, or why.*

"The one sure thing is you're a gloomy devil," Mackie Loudon said. But she said it with affection, being so much in control this morning that the demonic bickering was as pleasant to her as a choir. "You've always got the wrong idea," she said to Azazael. "You're my unnecessary demon." She moved the chisel and another pale peel of the outer wood came falling away from its dark core.

Mackie Loudon was headed home from a foraging expedition, her shoulders pulled down by the two plastic shopping bags that swung low from the end of her arms. Her head was lowered also and she scanned the pavement ahead of her for anything of interest that might be likely to appear. A couple of feet above the nape of her neck, Eliel and Azazael invisibly whirled around each other, swooping and darting like barn swallows at evening. They were having one of the witless arguments to which immaterial beings are prone, about whether or not it was really raining. It was plain enough to Mackie Loudon that it *was* raining, but not hard enough for her to bother stopping to take out the extra plastic bag she carried to tie around her head when it was raining hard. There were only a few fat raindrops splattering down, spaced far apart on the sidewalk.

She had almost come to the line of people shuffling into the matinee at the President Theater when she halted and sank to one knee to reach for a cloudy blue glass marble wedged in a triangular chip in the pavement. Just then there was some commotion in the movie crowd, and she looked up as a little black girl not more than five ran out into the street weeping and screaming, with a fat black woman chasing her and flogging her across the shoulders with a chain dog leash, or so Azazael began to maintain.

Did you see that? hissed Azazael, his voice turning sibilant as it lowered. On the street a car squealed to a sudden halt, blasted its horn once and then drove on. The line had reformed itself and the tail of it dragged slowly into the theater's lobby.

See what? said Eliel. *None of these people look like they saw anything....*

They never see, said Azazael. *That's the way of the world, you know.*

Mackie Loudon grasped the marble with her thumb and forefinger and held it near her stable eye, but it had lost its luster. The cloud in it looked no longer like a whirlwind, but a cataract. She flipped the marble over the curb and watched it roll through a drain's grating.

Are you deaf and dumb and blind? Azazael was carping. *Don't you know what happens to children nowadays?*

"SHUT UP!!" Mackie Loudon cried as she arose and caught up her bags. "Both of you, now, you just *shut up*." On the other side of the street an ancient man who'd been dozing in a porch swing snapped his head up to stare at her.

In the bedroom was a low bed with a saggily soft mattress, and whenever Mackie Loudon retired she felt it pressing in on all sides of her like clay. But if she woke in the middle of the night, she'd find herself sucked out through a rip in the sky, floating in an inky universal darkness, the stars immeasurably distant from herself and one another, and a long, long way below, the blue and green Earth reduced to the size of a teardrop. Somewhere down there her husband, son and a pair of grandchildren (that she knew of) continued to exist, and she felt wistful for them, or sometimes felt an even deeper pang.

You chose us, sang Eliel and Azazael. Out here, they always joined in a chorus. Out here, she sometimes thought she almost saw them, bright flickerings at the edges of her eyes. *And look, it's even more beautiful than you ever hoped it would be.*

"Yes, but it's lonely too," Mackie Loudon said.

You chose us, the demons droned, which was the truth, or near it.

Medusa wasn't going well; Azazael's objections were gaining ground, or somehow something else was wrong. Mackie Loudon couldn't quite make out what was the matter. She wandered away from the unfinished carving and her mind wandered with her, or sometimes strayed. As she passed along the dairy aisle at the A & P, small hands no bigger than insect limbs reached from the milk cartons to pluck at the hairs of her forearm. She wasn't sure just where or why but she suspected it had happened before, similar little tactile intimidations grasping at her from brown paper sacks or withered posters stapled to the phone poles.

Oh, you remember, Azazael was teasing her. *You can remember any time you want.*

"No, I *can't*," Mackie Loudon said petulantly. Across the aisle, a matron gave her a curt look and pushed her cart along a little faster.

Never mind, Eliel said soothingly. *I'll remember for you. I'll keep it for you till you need it, that's all right.* And it was true that Eliel did remember everything and had forgiven Mackie Loudon for it long ago.

There was a boy standing in the alley when Mackie Loudon set her garbage down, just a little old boy with a brush of pale hair and slate-colored eyes and a small brown scab on his jaw line. He wore shorts and a T-shirt with holes and he stood still as a concrete jockey; only his eyes moved slightly, tracking her. Mackie Loudon straightened up and put her hands on her hips.

"Are you real?" she said to him.

The boy shifted his weight to his other leg. "Why wouldn't I be?" he said.

"Hmmph," Mackie Loudon said, and put her head to one side to change her angle on him.

"Lady, your yard sho is a mess," the boy said. "The front yard and the back yard both."

"You're too little to cut grass yet a while," she said. "Lawnmower'd chew you up and spit you out."

"Who's that?" the boy said, and raised his arm to point at the house. Mackie Loudon's heart clutched up and she whipped around. It was a long time since anyone other than she had looked out of those windows. But all he was pointing at was a plaster bust she'd set on a sill and forgotten so well it was invisible to her now.

"Oh, that's just Paris," she said.

"Funny name," the boy said. "*Real* good-looking feller, though."

"He was a fool and don't you forget it," Mackie Loudon said in a sharper tone.

"Well, who was he, then?"

"Question is, who are *you?*"

"Gil mostly just calls me Monkey."

"That's not much name for a person," Mackie Loudon said. "What's your real name, boy?"

The child's face clouded over and he looked at the gravel between his feet.

"Won't tell, hey?" Mackie Loudon said. "All right, I'll just call you Preston. You answer to that?"

The boy raised his eyes back to her.

"All right, Preston, you drink milk?"

"Sometime, not all the time," Preston said.

"You eat cookies, I expect?"

"*All* the time," Preston said, and followed her up the steps into the house. She blew a small dried spider from a water-spotted glass and gave him milk and a lotus seed cake from a white waxed bag of them. Preston looked strangely at the cake's embossed and egg-white polished surface before he took a bite.

"What do you think?" Mackie Loudon said. She had poured an inch of cold coffee into her mug and was eating a lotus seed cake herself.

"I don't know, but it ain't a cookie," Preston said, and continued to eat.

"It's sweet, though, right? And just one will keep you on your feet all day. And do you know the secret?"

"Secret?"

"Got *thousand-year-old egg yolk* in it," Mackie Loudon said. "That's what puts the kick in it for you."

Preston bugged his eyes at her and slid down from his seat. He laid a trail of crumbs into the parlor, where she found him crouched on the desiccated carpet, lifting a corner of the sheet she used to veil Medusa.

"Ooooooo, *snakes*," said Preston, delighted. Mackie Loudon pulled his hand away so that the sheet fell back.

"Let that alone, it's not done yet," she said. "It's got something wrong with it, I can't tell what."

Preston turned a circle in the middle of the room, pointing at heads on the mantel and the bookcases.

"Who's that?" he said. "And that? And that?"

"Just some folks I used to know," Mackie Loudon told him. "But didn't you want me to tell you about Paris?" When Preston nodded, she took a lump of plasticine from an end table drawer and gave it to him to occupy his hands, which otherwise seemed to wander. Half consciously, he kneaded the clay from one crude shape to another, and his eyes kept roving around the room, but she could tell that he was listening closely. She started with the judgment of Paris and went on and on and on. Preston came back the next morning, and within a couple of weeks she'd started them into the Trojan War. By first frost they were on their way with the *Odyssey*.

The demons kept silent while Preston was there, and were quieter than usual even after he'd left. Azazael did a little griping about how the boy was wasting her time, but he had nothing to say with any real bite to it. Eliel was rather withdrawn, since he was much occupied with the task of observing Gil through Mackie Loudon's eyes and storing up in memory all he saw.

Preston lived with Gil in a house right next to Mackie Loudon's. The paint was peeling off the clapboards in long curly strips, and on the front door was a red and blue decal of a skull cloven by a zigzag lightning bolt. The windows, painted shut for a decade, were blacked out day and night with dirty sheets, behind which strange bluish lights were sometimes seen to flash in one room or another. There was no woman living there, though every so often one would visit, and sometimes little gangs of other scroungy children would appear and remain for a day or several, though the only one there permanently was Preston.

Gil himself was tall and stooped, with thinning black hair and not much chin. He affected motorcycle garb, though it didn't suit him. He was thin as from some wasting disease, and the boots and black leather and studded arm bands hung slackly from him like the plumage of some mangy kind of buzzard. He drove a newly customized black van with its rear windows cut in the shape of card-deck spades. He never seemed to go out to work, but he dealt in prodigious quantities of mail, getting and sending rafts of big brown cartons. Mackie Loudon would have thought he trafficked in drugs or other, bulkier contraband if she cared to think about it at all, but all these notions had been assumed by Eliel ever since the first time Gil had come to her door to fetch Preston. "Come out, Monk," he'd said through the mail slot, his voice whiny and insinuating. "Time to come along with Gil..." And she and the demons had seen the thousand tiny gates behind Preston's lips and eyes slide shut.

Preston loved the *Iliad*, the *Odyssey*, he loved the story of Perseus and the Gorgon, though he flinched a little at Diana and Acteon, but he didn't want to hear one word of Jason and the Argonauts. Indeed, at the first mention of the name a wracking change came over him, as if he'd been...possessed. He paled, he shook, he formed a fist of sharp white knuckles and smashed the little plasticine figure Mackie Loudon had made to represent the hero. Then he was out the back door and running pell-mell down the alley.

Azazael was back in a flash. *What did I tell you?* he suggested. *There's something in this setup that is really, really queer.*

"Children take these fits sometimes," Mackie Loudon said, for Azazael's remark was only typical of the weak and cloudy innuendos he'd been uttering through that fall. She turned to Eliel for confirmation, but for some reason Eliel didn't seem to be around.

Preston didn't come back for a week or more, but on the fifth day Gil came by to fetch him just the same. Mackie Loudon surprised herself by opening the door. Gil stood on the lower step, fidgeting with a dog's training collar, the links purling from hand to hand in a way that obscurely put her in mind of something disagreeable.

"The Monkey with you?" Gil said.

"That's no name for a human child," Mackie Loudon said. "And no, I hadn't seen him in a long time."

Gil nodded but didn't shift himself. He stretched the chain taut, its end rings strung on his middle fingers, then shut it between the palms of his hands.

"Didn't know you had a dog," Mackie Loudon said.

"Hee hee," said Gil. The front of his yellowing teeth was graven in black.

"Does that boy belong to you?"

Gil smiled again with his rotten teeth. "Yes, I believe you could say that," he said. "His skinny little butt is mine." He tossed the clump of chain and caught it with a jingle. "Old woman, I wouldn't suggest you meddle," he said, and turned to look back toward the street. "Nobody cares what goes on around here." He withdrew down the weedy walk, his feet slipping loosely in his outsize boots. Reluctantly, she followed him a little way, and when she stopped to look about her she saw that what he said was true. The houses on the block were held by knaves or madmen, or by no one. The lawns were dead, the trees were dying, a frigid wind blew garbage down the center of the street. From half the houses, broken windows overlooked her like sockets in a row of hollowed skulls.

On a cold blue morning Preston came to stand in the alley below the house again. For the first time Mackie Loudon noticed he didn't have a winter coat. She had to go and take his hand and lead him, to get him to come in. Though he seemed glad to see her, he wouldn't say a word. He sat in his usual wooden chair in the kitchen and stared at the pendulum swing of his feet.

"Cat got your tongue, has it?" Mackie Loudon said, and placed a yellow bean cake on the table near his hand. She went to the refrigerator for the milk she'd bought the day before, in some demonic premonition of his return, poured a glass and set it by him, took the carton back. In the light of the refrigerator's yellowed bulb she saw the faint blue photograph smeared on the carton's wall, and looked at it, and looked at Preston, and looked at the carton again. A line of blue letters crawled under the picture: *Jason Sturges of Birmingham, eight years old and missing since...* She shut the door and leaned on it and breathed before she turned to him.

"My God, boy," she said at last. "Do you know who you are?" And though the child didn't answer her, Eliel came back from wherever he'd been hiding and all at once returned to her the burden of her perception and her memory.

You blew it, Azazael snapped at her. *You bungled everything, like usual.*

Why couldn't you have just kept still a little longer? Eliel said. *God knows you stayed quiet long enough.* Mackie Loudon didn't answer them. She stalked from room to room, banging into the door jambs and the furniture. It was a long time since they'd been so angry with her, especially in concert, but she knew that they were justified. Preston, Jason, had bolted from the house the moment she'd asked that stupid question; she hadn't been quick enough to catch him. After that she'd called the police, called them once, called them twice –

That was pretty stupid too, Azazael said. *Everything considered, that might have been your worst move yet.* Mackie Loudon whirled on the parlor carpet and clawed one hand through the blank space where his voice came from. The Argonauts' little wooden ship crunched under her shoe; she booted its doomsaying figurehead into a corner. She went to her window and thumbed back a corner of the blind. Across the way, Gil's house hulked in the gathering twilight. It had taken the police all day and many calls to come – *All for nothing,* Eliel snapped. She had watched them come up to the porch and confer with Gil for a minute or two in the doorway and then leave.

"Goddamn," Mackie Loudon said, and let the blind fall back. She walked to the room's center and whipped the sheet off her Medusa. *What's the point?* said Azazael. She regarded the wooden expression of the broad blank face. The blunt heads of the snakes were blind because she'd never made their eyes. *No power there,* Eliel said sadly.

Mackie Loudon flung the chisel that had come into her hand; it stuck between Medusa's eyes and sagged. She was on Gil's board-sprung porch, pounding so heavily on the door that she almost fell forward when he snatched it from under her hand.

"The meddling old bat," Gil said contemplatively. "The *crazy* old bat, as the cops would say."

"Where's that boy?" Mackie Loudon said.

Gil raised one hand directly above the bald spot on his head and snapped his fingers once.

"Gone," he said. He made a plopping sound with his loose lips. "You understand, he just had to go."

"What did – "

"Never you mind," Gil said, and his face hardened. He stepped across the door sill and shoved her in the chest with the butt end of his palm. His arm was weak and reedy looking, but somehow it sent her staggering a long way back, down the porch steps into the littered yard. A slow fine drizzle sifted into her hair from the dark sky.

"I *told* you not to meddle," Gil said, and gave her another skinny little shove. "What good do you think it did anybody? The *police* say I should let them know if you *harass* me." He went on talking and pushing but Mackie Loudon wasn't really listening anymore. She was wondering what had happened to her strength. Her arms had always been powerful but now she couldn't seem to lift them, she couldn't speak a single word, and her legs seemed ready to give way and dump her on the matted grass and mud.

"I'm telling you, old bat," Gil said. "You want to stop messing in my business altogether." He gave her a two-handed shove and she went over the edge of the embankment. She tumbled down and cracked the back of her head on the sidewalk, hard enough to jumble her vision briefly, though it didn't knock her out. She lay with her left hand hanging off the curbstone, knuckles down. The rain fell into the corners of her open eyes. The quarreling demonic voices spiraled up and up away from her until they left her all alone in the silence of a vacuum, empty even of a single thought. Two or three people passed her by before anyone bothered to try and pick her up.

"Oh Mackie, Mackie," Nurse Margaret said from the height of her burnt-clay six foot two. Her hair was pinned back so tight under the white cap that it seemed to pull her sorrowing eyes even wider. "You last left here, you were talking so loud and walking so proud, I hoped to never see you back." Under Mackie Loudon's nose she shook two pills, one fire-engine red, one robin's-egg blue, but Mackie Loudon would not take her medication. She would not use her skills in craft class. She would not go to therapy group, she would not interact with anyone. She would not even speak a word. She would not. She would not.

With the demons gone the interior silence was deep indeed but Mackie Loudon was not aware of it. Human voices were distant and as completely unintelligible as the noise of the crickets in the grass. She let herself be herded from point to point on the ward, moving like an exhumed corpse made to simulate animation by a programmed sequence of electric shocks. She sat on a sprung couch in the dayroom and moved no more than a ledge of rock. All on its own her left eye opened and shut its lizard lid. An orderly pushed a mop before her, up and down, up and down. Behind her was the slap of playing cards and a mumble of voices blended into the static that came from the untuned TV. The season's changes appeared on the shatter-proof glass of the front window as if projected on a screen.

"Mackie Lou! Mackie Lou!" She heard, but it had been a long time since she'd recognized her name or any variation on it. A bluish plume of flame flashed up toward the darkened ceiling and went out. She sat up suddenly and turned. Two beds away in the long row, Little Willa was springing up and down on her mattress. Normally they tied her in; how had she got loose? But everything that happened next was even more improbable.

126

"Mackie Lou! Watch me, watch me, Mackie Lou!" Little Willa stopped her simian bounce, squirted a stream of lighter fluid into her mouth and blew sharply across a match she'd struck. Another compact fireball rolled in midair toward the doorway, illuminating the trio of orderlies who came near to knocking one another down in their haste to pin Little Willa to the floor and stuff her arms into restraints and haul her kicking and shouting from the room.

"Watch me, Mackie Lou!" But the demonic voices drowned her out. Azazael and Eliel were back, furiously arguing over the implications of what they'd seen, yammering so fast she couldn't follow them. They jabbered at incomprehensible speed, but after an hour, when they'd come to some agreement, they slowed down and turned to her again.

We've got a notion for you, said Eliel. *We've thought of a way for you to solve your problem.*

Mackie Loudon gave her head a long sad shake against the pillow. "You're not even real," she said.

You know better, said Azazael.

"Well. But you can't *do* anything."

Maybe not, said Eliel. *But watch us show* you *how to do it.*

"All right," she said. "At least I'll hear you out." And she listened meekly and attentively until almost dawn. As usual she got up with the others, shuffled in a line of others to receive the breakfast tray. But once they'd been sent into the dayroom, she called for Nurse Margaret and asked for her pills and began one more of her miraculously swift recoveries.

It was spring when Mackie Loudon was released and the weeds were knee deep in her yard, but in the house nothing was much changed. She did a meager bit of dusting, then plucked the chisel from between Medusa's eyes, licked her thumb and moistened the wounded wood. After a long considering moment, she went to the bedroom and snatched a big mirror loose from the closet door and propped it on a parlor chair. The reflection reversed all her movements, making her tend to cut herself as she worked. It took her the rest of the day to get the hang of it, and she stayed up with it through the night, but by next morning it was done and she wasn't even tired yet.

She taped her cuts and made herself a breakfast of dried mushrooms and dried minnows, drank a pot of coffee, had a spoon or two of pickled vegetables. She found her bottle of linseed oil and gave the finished carving a light anointment, then covered it once more with the sheet. When she closed her eyes and concentrated she felt her strong pulse striking tiny hammer blows; she felt the Gorgon visage pushing out on her brow as if embossed upon a shield. With care, she brushed her hair down over her forehead and went out.

In the shed that faced the alley there was a lawnmower which, though rusted, looked as if it would probably run. She dragged it around to the front yard, then carried a gas can down to a filling station two blocks over and had it filled. At a neighboring hardware store she bought a three-foot crowbar, and came home with this awkwardly balanced load. She was cutting the front lawn when Gil came out and did a double take.

"Well, if it ain't the old bat back," he said, shouting over the noise of the engine. Mackie Loudon gave him a cheerful wave and went on with her mowing. Cut ends of the tough privet stumps whirred around her head. Gil stared and shook his head and went down to his van. When its hind end had turned a corner, Mackie Loudon shut the mower off and went in her front door and out the back, collecting the crowbar on the way. One good jab and pry was good enough to break the flimsy lock on Gil's back door. She went in and softly shut the door behind her.

In Gil's front room a video camera watched her from the gloom, like an insect eye extended on a stalk. A light flick from the crowbar's tip shattered the lens into fine glass dust. She went through the whole house that way, smashing the cameras and enlargers, gouging out the works of the projectors and video decks with the hooked end of the crowbar. She didn't look at the tapes or the films, but she couldn't help seeing the big still prints, which showed children with children, children with grown-ups, children with assorted animals, a few children being tortured and killed.

They sowed bones, said Eliel, and Azazael answered. *They'll have their harvest.*

She didn't have long to wait for Gil, not much more than the time it took her to prepare. There was a two-gallon bucket under his sink, which she took empty to her house and brought back full. She dipped herself a ration in a mug and set it on a chair arm. Gil's key was turning in the lock; she stooped and hoisted the bucket. His eyes slid greasily around the wreck of his equipment, and he made a quick move toward her, but once she tossed the bucket on him he stopped, perplexed, and sniffed. She took the butane lighter from the patch pocket on her dress and with her other hand pulled back her hair to reveal the Gorgon. Gil's hands had just come up in supplication when he was turned to stone. She took a good swig from the mug and flicked the lighter's little wheel. A long bright tongue of fire stretched out and drew him wholly in.

It was a windless day and the house burned all alone, flames rising vertically into the cloudless blue sky. The firemen came, the police came, they blocked off either end of the street and soaked the roofs of the nearby houses, but there was nothing of the burning house to save. The people came out of the houses that were not yet abandoned and stood on the sidewalks with folded arms and grimly watched it burn. Mackie Loudon stood in her half-cut yard, leaning on the mower for support. Her other arm was tightly wrapped around herself, because in spite of the spring weather and the fire's harsh heat she was feeling very cold. She waited to be taken into custody, but no one seemed to notice her at all, and when the fire had fallen into its own embers, she went into her house and shut the door.

....Madison Smartt Bell

This Side of the Wall

Sometime they'll give a war and nobody will come.
– Carl Sandburg

Nineteen, and reflected alone in dark marble
the polished black wall stretches hungrily
and I tumble back thirteen years
to the very same place, where at six years old
I sat cross legged in the grass and watched
the sun dancing with the cherry leaves

19 years before, a boy decided it would be easier
to put a bullet through his left foot
than face the jungle at night.

The night belonged to Charlie.

I was still learning my alphabet
and stared at the glorious tumble of letters
chiseled in dark marble
and scattered with roses.

Papa, you must have made a handsome soldier.

In a small wooden box in the corner of the basement,
a snapshot,
my father playing checkers on a pile of sandbags,
his helmet in his lap,
one hand on a rifle

At six years old I watched his reflection stare back at him
until I couldn't tell which side of the black marble he belonged on.
with a gasp I took his hand
just to be sure.

His thumb ran deliberately over a line of letters
wiping away where tears should have been.
"He was my best friend."
he whispered, eyes heavy and unmoving

At six years old the wall of letters became words
and words became names
                    became fathers
                            holding hands with could-have been daughters
    who will never learn the alphabet
      or the sun in the cherry leaves

At six years old through the thick smell of sun warmed flowers
a nightmare
rolled tightly in olive drab
and tucked away in my father's bottom drawer
unfolded freshly in me

They left my father for dead with a hole in his chest
in mud so stagnant it rotted his toenails

In the bedroom of a six-year-old girl
with cinnamon braids falling across a pillowcase printed with roses
the night again belonged to Charlie.

My father spent his 21st birthday pissing on himself
in a foxhole curled up like a baby
crying for his mother and
begging for his life
from any god he could dream of.

When I'm tipsy in a short skirt
dancing to Happy Birthday
with a beer in my hand and a friend on each arm
I will remember
and thank those same gods for my
enduring innocence

.....*Kathryn Lange*

my diRtY SaVIoR

The burning bush doesn't mean much anymore.
The neighbor's children are playing with matches again.
The water from the rock we had to filter
In order to remove the dangerous bacteria.
So what if you believe that it's the body and the blood?
When everything is proven and nothing is believed
Our minds begin to wander
And we slowly turn to a different savior.
He writes our music and parades it as our own.
He reads us stories he has written to fill us with himself.
He paints us pictures in our minds and barters them for souls.
And we listen to the music, and we study all the stories,
And we see his pretty pictures, and we want to believe.
He becomes our work and our home,
He becomes our night and our day,
He becomes our life and our Death.
Corrupt, ancient, cunning, weak,
He is our dirty savior.
Why do we need an obsolete trinity
When a god with a billion faces can bring us sweetness and addiction?
As he slips deep inside our fragile skin
The spirit blesses us in silver
While Jesus bleeds green on the cross.

.... Brian Wood

Bismillah

Let's break bread together.
Let's break challah.
When we break it let's say *bismillah*
which means *in God's name.*
For when the Lord has torn and
healed your heart
you will never be the same.
This bread is braided
the way we are all woven into one.
This bread is made with eggs.
To serve the Lord forever more
is all I'll ever beg of my mother.
She is none other than the same true God.
I thank her for my birth
and my work and my rest
and this bread.
I thank her for the sweet green earth
my feet are blessed to tread.

....*Robert Francis Strott*

The number 2000 isn't any more important than the number 1960 was when it came after 1959, or than 1900 was when it came after 1899. The rules, it seems to me, the rules of what it means to be a good human — to be giving and righteous and good — don't change simply because the numbers do.

....Edward P. Jones

A serious shift from the need for endless acquisition that marks the "consumer culture" of the industrialized world at the end of the 20th century, toward praise and thanks, could help open our minds and hearts to respond with care to the pain — of people and of the planet — that also marks this millennial time on the planet. In a culture of praise, we might begin to truly face the injustice deeply present on our planet and move to heal it. A culture marked by praise, with heart and mind open to healing pain — this is a culture that I dream of helping to make. This is a culture that poets and writers have the power to help us all make.

....Sara Ebenreck

Rural Maryland

In rural Maryland I mistook a barn
for a church.
Painted white with long, vertical windows.
A spiritual place surrounded by tall grass.

The September brown field.

Nearby, the transcendent smoke
my blue emotion
rose from a small chimney.

.....Alan Britt

The Thrower of Stones

"He threw a stone," Mother said,
decades after Grandfather was buried,
"across the fishpond and killed his brother."
He threw a stone, he was nine or ten,
playing in the family courtyard in Sin Wei,
our ancestral village in China. He had been told
to look after his little brother. He was
keeping him amused, slinging stones
in their ornamental pool
to fool the fish into rising for food.
The sun was shining, it was the morning
of his life, a morning like any morning,
with nothing to do except disturb
the equilibrium of carp and koi
by making ripples with the gravity of stones.
He was proud of his strength, impatient
with his brother's short tosses.

"Watch me!" he called across the circular
cement wall that held fish and water in place.
He pulled back his arm and sent his strength
into the stone, saw it arc through air, saw
the unspeakable, unstoppable landing,
the sudden released red
in his brother's forehead.
All at once the sunlight was too bright,
his ears lost the ability to hear.
His eyes could not blink.
Images burned into the darkness,
the exposed negatives behind his eyes:
his brother's puckering brow,
the slow toppling of the body over
the cement wall, into the dark water.

His hearing returned with the splash
and the shadows, large and small,
weaving and dancing about the pale form.
He saw his brother's hand wave
as if to say, "Follow me, the water's cool."
Reason later knew it had been just
the refraction of light and moving water.
Reason could explain, it could not
stop his vision, always the red hole
in that forehead, the silent (it is always
silent) falling and then, the splash of
displaced water, the pale hand moving
sluggishly as if tired, overcome by sleep.

Grandfather never knew the story of Cain
and Abel, but he left China, lived out his days
in an alien land. For what he had done,
even though accidentally, exile, instinct told him,
was the only bearable solution.

.....*Hilary Tham*

Primer

Hands. eyes. mouth. nose. teeth
Smile. knees. ankles. feet,
Walk. At two, I learn
"my" alphabet. My
hands. My feet. My face.
My teeth, nose, eyes, on
and on. I recite words
out loud then find the shape –
matchings like socks. Each
sound, a mirror of outward
appearance, like pant legs, always two:
two eyes two hands two lips – one mouth
speaks and learns things are
as they exist. And my compact
vocabulary builds into dictionaries I must
abandon, forget in another season,
when births of the spirit teach my body
that things are not only as they exist:
      simile, symbol, metaphor, irony.
I know now that I am born
to lose my body only, not the shared
with you, dearest comrade –
smiles, evoked from Heart's hidden stirrings, moving

       like leaves on meditations' winds – and if lucky – I learn,
we are born, Contingent, born into a new
alphabet of knowledge, ancient and sacred:
       learn Gardens, whose blossoms
are not here only, but blooming
invocations to Invisible Becoming,
to the Unknowable. And so this
is all I am now, friend: Poetry, Spirit –
       And Prayer: My eyes, my hands,
mouth....
       Clothed by Love, I
walk back into Eden, unafraid,
with you.

....Donna Denizé

Freedom Ride

from the back of the bus
I can hear the wind outside
splashing against the hull

of seats as if this was the
shores of Africa during rush
hour and the slave trade is

steered by a driver who never
learned the words to Amazing
Grace

bless me Father for knowing
the difference between unemployment
and freedom

bless me Father for replacing
chains with change and tokens
and transfers

bless me Father for this window
which turns away the stares
and the eyes filled with despair

bless me Father
as I sit here in the back of
the bus wondering about the

absence of your power and presence

....E. Ethelbert Miller

I hear a woman's voice
Without looking I know it is Mary Nelson.
I hear her voice,
            Bless us, O Lord, and these, our gifts

and I want to just sit and listen

because that's the blessing my family says
            that's the blessing my family has said
                every night we have eaten a meal together
                    in restaurants, at campground picnic tables, at our table
                that's the blessing that each of us still say silently
                    even when we are apart

apart

like Mary Nelson is, in the mental hospital.

eating her lunch in a room full of people
who have slit marks on their wrists,
who hear voices, who have bruises
under their eyes

She says this blessing
And she says the blessing out loud.

I don't turn to look at her
but I can see her smile
because maybe she's thinking,
like I am

of all the blessings said with our own families
holding hands around the table
feeling each others' skin
as we

give thanks

for these, our gifts.

.....*Anne McCauley*

Altar Piece

The roses should be large enough that you
can see them from far away. Then
they should be long-stemmed and blood-red.
Their color will reflect on the walls and tint
the dusty sunlight in its farthest corner.
They will draw all eyes forward, not to their petals,
or to their green leaves, but to their thorns and to their waxy
cool stems. The odor of the roses will resemble human skin.
It will be heavy, not sweet, and it will reach you
before you see the flowers. It will make you think
of someone you had forgotten. It will be overpowering so
that you will hear the dead pray. Beside
this magnificence, the figure on the cross will look as disreputable
as ever, and you will pity Him.
This will bring the roses closer.

....Diane Scharper

What stories are supposed to do is open doors. They allow directions for people to go.

.....*Wayne Karlin*

Both writing and reading literature well often requires a descent into places we don't want to go. But when we genuinely explore our stories, we are able to come to the universal and thus we begin to understand the bridges that connect us.

.....*Maria Mazziotti Gillan*

Evolution of Marriage

Her body and his, as if music created
their fit at that perfect, impossible

angle; the blades
of their skates dueling
the ice like a knife dance.

Husband and wife
exiled by desire to the frontiers
of gravity, their lives

in the balance. What beyond love
impelled him to hurl her spiraling

into the red flame
of her hair, to the thin edge
of her returning.

As if his arm were an altar,
she lay on the air. And I believed

that the actual substance of our bodies
is the size of a fingernail.

That we are space
shaped and reshaped by molecular
lightening.

They mated before my eyes like airborne
butterflies and I wondered

what new species
they are creating; how much further
flesh can thin into wings.

....Karen E. Zealand

Because I Didn't Take The Picture

for Rebecca

February 28, 1985, Fairmont, West Virginia.
The plain motel stands in front of you,
the rolling, snow-patched WVA farmlands,
a few distant cows and a picnic table behind.
A gallon of red jug wine colors the gray
scene. You stand and laugh with the others,
plastic cups toasting the frozen air.
Pete looks for all the world like Ferdinand
Marcos with a silly wool cap pushed on his head;
Jim looks like my father in fatter days;
Tom looks not quite like anyone except, perhaps,
a linebacker or someone's nearly forgotten cousin;
and you look as you'll always look to me,
like those pictures from your childhood, a sly
sidelong glance at whoever took the picture.
You tell me to take the picture;
I leave the camera in its box.
Now, in some bottomless future, no one
need wonder whose faces those were smudging
the unplacable landscape; no one need guess
our ages when the shutter clicked or try to date
us by our clothes, invent lives for us they wish
they'd had. Now they'll know who and where
we were that day so long ago and they'll know
it was I who wrote this, the real picture.

...James Taylor

145

Sunday Afternoon

for my brothers

Rolling into a patch of sunlight
laughing without reason
spreading the scent of summer grass
over our similar bodies
we are caught in agelessness.
Inside the dark house
our father is arguing.
He placed his joy of life
and eyes of discovery
into our making.
We golden haired children
are tumbling
from shadow to sunlight
in a stranger's yard
trying to share this gift
help him remember
the caressing itch
of grass meeting skin
and the yellow green
perfume of abandon.

.....Lara Payne

Fat Is In Fashion

When he was young, slender as a rich man,
never in my wildest did I think Bondurant
would someday win the belly-butting
contest at the tobacco festival.
You know how it goes? They whitewashes
a circle in the dirt, and matches guys up
according to height. My old Duranty was
in the five-foot six and under group.
Arching his back, pooching out his gut,
he butted ever single person in his class
to hell and back and out of the circle.
Ladies kindly give credit to my
buttery cooking, but in my insides,
secret heart, I know nasty old Stroh's
what's give him that seven month pregnancy
what never gets ready to deliver.
In spite of booze, he's still strong
and hard as a bad woman's expression.
City folk, with their flimsy, slim ways,
can't understand that weight gives a man
a feeling of importance when Lady Luck
is passing him by just like it did all
them poor folks what went before him.
I'm proud of my man's belly, just like
he's proud of my big, hanging boobs.
Like gold medals dangling for everbody
to see, is proof that I filled them
babies we made, year after loving year.

.....Marie Kennedy Robins

On Being a Witness at My Husband's Citizenship Hearing

Reliable as any wife,
I solemnly certify the moral fitness
of my husband. What is a citizen
if not loyal? I swear
he's always been able to support
himself, never broke a law on that long list,

that, as far as I know, he's not communist.
This judge suspects an alien inner life –
trouble spots not on the passport
to which I must have access.
I suppose I could mention the underwear
scissored from silken

antelope hide. How his yen
for certain customs in bed persists.
How unfamiliar his tint of hair
still is. How wild language survives
in his sleep like a goddess
so that his waking is, well, an effort –

all the dark evidence he didn't report.
But no. I'll continue to spy and listen
I confess
with the subversive joy of a pacifist.
I want my arms around other lives
that would, in a different dream, keep me scared.

The judge will compare
him to the solid home born sort,
will contrive
to remodel the nature I've chosen
to love. Though I'm no purist
I confess

I too have longed to possess
that stranger. When stuck in the solitaire
of my tribal dream, I tried to insist
on full disclosure, as though I could convert
the deepest language of another. I was mistaken.
We are ourselves, no matter how far we live
                          from home.

....Karen Sagsetter

Breadbaker at Night

Drowsing yeast yawns awake
in milk and blackstrap,
humble as its blue-striped bowl.
While I sleep, that sponge grows,
until, full of itself,
it is risen.

Silent, he works the yeast
into unsifted flour,
coarse with its bran.
Now, as one, yeast and flour
rise together.
By light of moon, his hands fold,
press, knead the living mass
and form it into loaves.
Mound by mound,
each panfull, its own bellows,
there is a second rising.
He lifts each on his paddle,
eases it into transforming heat.

Our oven crusts each loaf,
restrains each resurrection,
insists the risen, this time,
shall be bread.

....Marguerite Beck-Rex

Posthumous

Would it surprise you to learn
that years beyond your longest winter
you still get letters from your bank, your old
philanthropies, cold flakes drifting
through the mail-slot with your name?
Though it's been a long time since your face
interrupted the light in my door-frame,
and the last tremblings of your voice
have drained from my telephone wire,
from the lists of the likely, your name
is not missing. It circles in the shadow-world
of the machines, a wind-blown ghost. For generosity
will be exalted, and good credit
outlasts death. Caribbean cruises, recipes,
low-interest loans. For you who asked
so much of life, who lived acutely
even in duress, the brimming world
awaits your signature. Cancer and heart disease
are still counting on you for a cure.
B'nai Brith numbers you among the blessed.
They miss you. They want you back.

...Jean Nordhaus

The Ideal

As if their very comeliness were centrifugal,
we move back slightly from
the husband and wife standing together
under the outdoor lights of a summer party.
Tanned, vibrant, expressive, perfectly
proportioned, they make clear, unwittingly
and in relief, our ordinary, passably-attractive
selves. What is it like to stand among the less
well-formed, the simply plain with too short
or too long noses, jutting or receding chins
and all the other oddments of contour
and bulk that are the common human lot?
God and goddess, or king and queen, amassing
mythic energy as they speak and gesture,
they are sweet-tempered and thoughtful,
so the sentiment that they exist to diminish
the rest of us, quickly shows itself as jealousy.
We almost expect tragedy to befall them,
they are so unmarred, so near to perfection.
Perhaps they see themselves as less attractive
then they are, know one another's frailties,
foibles, late-night fears, and yet these forms
of model grace – body, face – must astound
and beguile each as they beguile us who relive,
sadly, standing before them, self-conscious
in the light, the long-buried dream we clung to
in our youth: one day we, too, would be beautiful.

....Gray Jacobik

Soundings
I. The Silent Treatment

It was the first week of junior high, first time in the big school, with its lockers, grownup schedules, and maze-like hallways streaming with strangers. We were in gym class, sitting around on the bleachers because we didn't have our uniforms yet and hadn't been formed into squads. A wiry tough named Floyd Rose passed quietly behind me and left a gob of phlegm on the back of my shirt.

No taunts. No guffaws. Only a cock of his slicked head, a bemused glint in his eyes, and a grin full of fine white teeth that promised danger.

I'm not sure how I would have reacted if my father hadn't started making suggestions that night. Probably I would have simply accepted this fear along with all the lesser anxieties of seventh grade, doing my best to avoid confrontations and hoping that my own harmlessness would make me immune to trouble.

I was raised, after all, on the story of Ferdinand the Bull, who dreamed not of butting heads or goring matadors but of sitting just quietly under his cork tree and smelling the flowers. Force was for brutes. My parents believed in building character with doses of the *New York Times* and Leonard Bernstein's Young People's Concerts.

As for dealing with bullies, the tale passed down from my father's boyhood in the Depression-era Bronx exalted psychology over bloodshed. When one of the neighborhood kids started picking on Dad, he and his brother responded with the Silent Treatment. They just ignored the tormenter; stared right past him. He ceased to exist. Provocation turned to exasperation and finally to pleading. All in vain. It got to the point where the kid's mother came weeping up to their apartment, begging my grandmother to intercede, please please tell Meyer and Irving to talk to Tony again. What a legend. It was my favorite story about the old days.

So I was surprised when the gob incident set my father to spinning out plans for actual battle. I should gather up my buddies, we should travel in a pack, let Floyd and his lackeys know that they were dealing not with a lone victim but with an alliance. And if it came to fighting, we could deal out a few black eyes of our own. Teach the bully a lesson.

I must say I was silently appalled. The idea of exchanging serious punches seemed unreal. Maybe I was a coward, maybe I was overly sheltered, but I couldn't imagine myself in a fistfight. The idea of enlisting my friends as a gang embarrassed me.

As it turned out, nothing happened. Evidently I didn't matter to Floyd nearly as much as he mattered to me. But my father's response stayed with me, sowing doubts, making me wonder about the power of civility – which Dad has always embodied – compared to the effectiveness of force, which he advocated at least that once, if only as a contingency.

Now my own sons are entering that no-man's-land between childhood and the grownup world, drifting away from me into a place over which I have no control and which they don't tell me much about anyway. I've always urged them to ignore teasers and bullies, and I've even passed along the story of the Silent Treatment, and they've always said to me, "That won't stop them," in a tone of voice, despairing, accusing, which suggests that I don't know anything about the real world.

Did the Silent Treatment really bring Tony down? Would fists have taught Floyd a lesson? It bothers me when my sons resist my suggestions. But what bothers me is not their resistance so much as my own feeling, and perhaps theirs, that a father is supposed to know what to do. He's supposed to be a moral hero. In that silent and skeptical realm where my sons now dwell, do they ever hear a guiding voice, or recall a legend, that comes from me?

In retrospect, I wonder if my own father was groping, equally unsure, beset himself by the assumption that a father is supposed to know what to do. If he gave me a mixed message, perhaps he was only reflecting a parent's frustration at having no control over the world that gapes darkly before his children.

Oddly enough, I had another close encounter with Floyd Rose, four years later, when we were both juniors on the high-school football team. He was still a greaser; I was still a student. He played first-string, though he wasn't quite as big as he should have been and would lose his starter's status the following year. I mostly sat on the bench. He showed no signs of remembering the gob; I had shelved the incident away, untroubled by it now but always knowing it was there.

One game day late in the fall, the two of us had suited up early and found ourselves out by the bleachers, alone. "I guess it's been a tough season for you," he said, gazing at the field. "You work really hard, but you don't get to play very much."

I was aware by that time that I would never be a football player. I lacked the confidence, the recklessness, the muscled reflexes. "I don't know," I told Floyd. "I'm not sure it's in me."

"Yeah," he said thoughtfully, "you gotta have the killer instinct." And he fell silent and looked out at the lined turf, fingering his helmet.

It was the only conversation we ever had. But it was that handful of words, I think – a brief exchange that ambushed us both in that moment before the hits and tackles began – that fixed the gob in my memory for the future. There was something delicate and decent in his tone, and almost sad, as if he already guessed that he wouldn't have enough bone and brawn to start next year. As if he knew that wiry wasn't enough. And as if he might be wondering himself about the killer instinct — whether he truly believed in it after all.

....Dan Laskin

Vines

Though you would get tough
in August, uproot garlands
of honeysuckle and ivy,

the vines never gave ground.
They circle through privet,
forsythia, around each other

the way marriage wound
a thicket over us, rambling
at first, branching with children,

resting between seasons.
I unravel wild trumpets
from wisteria,

pull down creepers
tangled on lilacs,
but can no longer tell

within our maze
which strands were mine,
which ones began with you.

....Elizabeth Follin-Jones

It's 4:00 a.m., black as death, and a boy is standing at our bedside. "Dad, I don't feel well. Can you come to my room?"

I wouldn't be completely honest if I didn't admit that my first reaction is "Oh, damn." But he looks so small and unhappy trudging ahead of me in the dark. I sigh and say, "What's the matter?"

"My chest hurts." A small stab of anxiety: this is something new.

We settle ourselves on his bed, side by side, staring up at the ceiling, and he asks, "What do you think it is?" I have no idea. A tumor? A rare heart disorder? The unknown spreads its arms over the dark room as we gaze upward. I wish I could tell him something, anything, for certain about the future.

"Is it a sharp pain or a dull pain?" I ask, buying time.

And then something occurs to me. He has just started playing the clarinet, and earlier tonight he was blowing furiously, cheeks ballooning, forcing hurricanes into the narrow black tube. I explain that he might have strained a muscle around his ribs; and, though I'm actually unsure whether the ribs even have muscles, I go on to say how I've heard of people who coughed so hard or even laughed so hard that they actually cracked a rib.

It sounds plausible, but he can tell I'm groping. "Are you making this up?" No, I assure him, and I blather on, skipping words over the surface of my fear in the hope that it will sink beneath their weight, until he interrupts me, bemused now, aware of my discomfort, and maybe bored as well. "It's okay, dad. It doesn't hurt anymore."

Thus reassured, I relax. We both relax. It's good to feel his safe warm body next to mine, and I think of when he was little and I could hold and heft him all the time, of the countless games we played, wrestling, rolling, when his whole body, his whole being would ride a father's frame. The best of those games, it comes to me now, was Bird Blow-Up; and, like all the best games, we invented it ourselves. Here is how you play:

You start out lying on your stomach, flat as a deflated balloon (which is, in fact, what you are pretending to be), with your son lying on top of you. He cups his hand to your back and starts to puff, blowing you up. Slowly you arch your back, rise to your knees, then to your legs, until he has successfully "inflated" you: you're a man-sized balloon, standing up now, with your son clinging piggy-back to your shoulders and neck.

You're airborne, both of you. You start to float around the house. It's clear that you're up in the sky because, as you move slowly down the hall, you're singing, in a high-pitched voice, "Floating along, floating along...what a beautiful view...just floating along."

You admire flocks of geese and soar over lakes, noticing the tiny boats and toy cottages below. Every so often, just for giggles, you hit some turbulence or barely miss a cliff. There's a hawk gliding over by the bookcase, quite beautiful. Your son tightens his grip as the hawk comes nearer, then nearer, and then you're shouting, "No, go away! Shoo!" and your son is laughing, and you're shaking, shouting "No, no, he's too close! He's going to peck us!" and your son is holding on tighter, and laughing harder, and suddenly, *Pop!*, "Help!" you're punctured, and with a buzzing, thoroughly vulgar blatting – the sound of the air escaping from dad – you start to spin wildly out of control as you break into a run down the hall with your son's laughter and shrieks mingling with the explosive rush of wind from your lips.

The rest of the game is a maniacal dash through the whole house. You bounce and bump and run, but most of all you spin. You are blatting the whole time, and your boy is totally simpled-out laughing. Your wife shouts, "Be careful!" by which she means, *Don't drop him, don't twist your ankle and fall, don't crack his skull against the wall, don't slip and tumble down the stairs with our son on your back*; and you dimly sense the presence of danger, too, as if a tiny inner knife were testing your fears, but you're having too good a time spinning and sputtering and hearing your son's helpless laughter.

And, as you spin, hilariously deflating with your son on your back, you're also dimly aware that someday your boy will be too heavy for this, or too old to want it, and you won't have the back for it anyway, or the knees, or the lungs. You're spinning, spinning and deflating, and you wonder – not in words, exactly – about all the terrible dangers in the world, and whether your son will survive them, and whether you will; and as you spin through the house, narrowly avoiding every collision in the onrush of uncontrollable laughter, you wonder whether your boy will have children of his own, and whether you'll know them, and whether all of you will float together someday on that lake by the cottage...spinning, and wondering, not in words but in the whirling of your bodies, as if motion were a kind of prayer.

And, finally, with a last spin and a desperate sputter, you're out of air and you crash on his bed, flat on your stomach. And there he is, still laughing, safe on your back. And when he stops laughing, he says, "Again." And he cups his hand and starts to puff, and tightens his grip. And so it begins all over again.

I smile as I lie there beside him, thinking about his ribs and the clarinet and Bird Blow-Up; thinking, *This at least is something I know about fatherhood.* And if I can pass along a bit of wisdom, it would be this: Lying in bed after a day of Bird Blow-Up with your boy, you may notice an aching in your chest.

Don't worry about it. It's normal.

....Dan Laskin

The Ghosts In Our Bed

to my husband
who has Early Onset Parkinson's Disease

The mahogany four-poster bed your mother left us
is high up off the floor. It folds us into
the smell of lavender in sheets sprinkled with violets
the thick blue and green comforter.
For years we are happy in it,
lusty and young and so alive together,
this safe place to which we return each night
to lie in each other's arms, warm and exactly
where we want to be.

Now, when we climb into our bed, those people
who for so many years were ourselves, the ghosts
that we live with, sleep between us.

You have become so fragile. You are always
cold and need extra blankets, and you sleep
so quietly, your arms folded across your chest,
that when I wake up in the night, I have to reach out
to find you because I'm not certain you're there.

You used to take up so much space, with your energy
and strength, the big bones of your body.
I pile blankets on you, now,
your face rigid and frozen even in sleep.
The ghosts of the future hover over us, reminding us
every night of how much more we have to lose,
even as our old ghosts whisper, "Remember, remember."
I fall asleep with my hand on your shoulder,
to keep you with me as long as I can.

....*Maria Mazziotti Gillan*

Anytown

"I told you to get in the car, damn it!"

This is a town of many kids and little patience,
of many trees and little time to watch the trees
sway when a wind blows up from the south,
under April sun, causing the kids to jump
and dart through the stripmall parking lot.

This is a town of many roads and little signs,
of many ways to go and little time to hear the clouds
course, in effortless banter, across the April sky,
causing the kids to jump and dart through
the stripmall parking lot.

This is a town of many trucks and little Fords,
of many yellow lights run and little time to smell
cut grass, the wet walks behind, under the sprinkler
causing the kids to jump and dart through
the stripmall parking lot.

This is a town of many moods and little dogs,
of many clocks and little time to taste the wild berries
shining darkly on the median, under the birthday
playland sign, causing the kids to jump and dart
through the stripmall parking lot.

This is a town of many parents and little kids,
of many ways to love and little time for these kids,
under their South Park tee shirts.

....Neal Dwyer

The Kind of Woman to Marry

November 13, 1998

Dear Josh and Eamon,

We didn't go to the islands or Paris on our honeymoon.
We went to Cape May, NJ, where the proprietor of a B&B refused
us shelter because we arrived at 3 a.m. after an all night drive.

That first night we slept on the beach by the nun's convent
near the lighthouse. It was freezing and my new bride (your mother)
and I clung to each other for warmth.

Since that night, many others have slammed doors in our
faces. Always, we've clung to each other near the outgoing tide
and laughed with each sunrise after the cold, harsh night.

> So marry a woman like that –
> one like your mother
> one who shelters you
> from the cold and dark
> both human and nature.

Love,

Dad

.... *Bruce Curley*

Morning Quatrains

for Ynez

When daylight arrived, shrouded
In the pretext of morning
Fog, I had almost forgotten what it was
I wanted to say.

Then soft air landed
On the balcony
Of pink and fuchsia impatiens,
The ones that seduce hummingbirds

Like clockwork each noon
As the sun crawls onto wooden planks,
Serene under shadows
Of black metal railings

Where warmth dances against my skin
And I am kissing my wife
Who is miles away
Charting the delicate flow

Of misguided hands,
How automobiles clash
As if bumblebees tangling
Over a bright yellow sunflower.

I want to tell her I'm safe,
That I miss her
Here, amid words gently colliding
Among the countless seedlings

That have now grown like children.
When I water them, I say,
"She'll be home around six."
And they always listen,

Drinking what I whisper,
Thoughts of her
Sinking into their roots,
As I turn them, I hear them sing her name.

...*Jeffrey Lamar Coleman*

Lydia

There was life before us

my sister and I discovered,
looking at photographs

we shouldn't have been looking at
of the English girl my father

was engaged to during the war.
Here she is right in front of our eyes,

the woman before my mother,
in a black lace cocktail dress,

a cigarette in a holder,
pensive, earthy – waiting

in front of the carved wooden radio,
for news from the front.

This is the war, after all,
and here she is again, somewhere

on an English beach, draped
across my father's shoulder

all of her silky skin radiant
above the soft folds of sun dress.

They stand in front of a sign
that reads "Seaside Cottages,

two dollars." And here she is
again, painted onto the cockpit

of my father's plane with hardly
anything on at all, and here he is

in his flight jacket, looking
in fact, happy. My sister and I each

lift our pencils like cigarettes,
taking long sultry drags to puff

out invisible rings. They rise
in the air like silver nooses

that will catch our father
and hold him to us.

....*Geraldine Connolly*

I think encounters with the natural world ask us to reconsider
whether beauty might have less to do with the picturesque and
more to do with intimacy and coherence and integrity.

....Barbara Hurd

Observation leads to reflection, then to introspection. If,
however, the process stops there, it is an empty quest. For if we
operate relationally, as the natural world teaches us, what
purpose does understanding ourselves serve if we do not extend
that further and work toward courtesy and caring for others,
binding our community together. Creative writers perhaps know
better than most that observation, reflection and caring require
time. And there is the vision that nature writing gives to me:
that it is worthwhile to take time to observe, ponder, and then
live that courtesy and respect which inspire others to care.

....Kate Chandler

Rolling Pennies

They're survivors; the room is rich
with their praise – a cloud of copper,
fragrant as boxwoods or incense.
They slide, 2-4-6-8-10, 2-4-6-8-20,
into a roll. The count grows into a chant
that takes my hands. This might be knitting,
but there won't be any thing in the end.
94's ching against those that wear
green tarnish like a beard.

Whose lint have they gathered?
Some, figuring in nickel bets, were passed
at playgrounds: "You can too see Lincoln
in the memorial." Or held in open palms,
spared from sacrifice on train tracks,
maybe in Eisenhower's second term.

At a 1960 I see a child catching
a glint of mica at the side of a road.
He held it to the light, barely breathing,
to read messages from the mineral world.
I slide that old penny into the roll,
a miner in reverse, and count.

....Sunil Freeman

Foxfire

A foxfire scattering of stars
and a lone planet hang low
over the northeast, where the wind
comes from, down like a coyote,
nose down, its warm tongue licking

a chill out of the earth, the dawn's
chill of stiff awakenings after
the night's dancers, their supple sweat,
the way it loves its body, then sinks
into salt rest. The earth last

night sank so, its blush and rose
twilight giving up the light so well
that those in their houses walked out
into the roads and yards, arms folded,
their skins flushed with an excitement

drawn of this pink light, and discussed
it – not the coyote's old trail
they stood on, but the huge
evanescent cathedral of light
that reared before them like a great

dancer, his headress streaming
its eagle wildness, while they talked
their awe of its wordless beauty.
The subtle dawn, alone with foxfire,
now reclaims. It licks the wounds

that words have made in us, that we
in that first step down made of ourselves.

...*J. H. Beall*

Why I Never Take Off My Watch at Night

(1)

Our dog, left home alone too long,
would worry all the things that held
the scent of my son – pajamas, a blanket,
socks, and once a baseball bat –
into a pile inside the front door.
He'd sleep on that pile in the dark
and wait for the right high pitch
of pistons ticking up our street.

(2)

Keep in touch, we tell the young men as we send them
off to our wars. Then the remote-controlled TV
tells us what they touch in their pockets:
a braid of hair, a plastic cross, the picture
of a girl, a tiny Bible, a smooth stone
from the crawl-space underneath the house.

(3)

I like to grope a little, scare myself
by crossing over borders without maps until
I do not know the language of the place.
I wear the smell of being lost
in ancient streets, connected to nothing
except a distant drum-tap
from the far red outpost of the wrist,
the thready little rhythm to go home to.

(4)

Sometimes when I sail, grey silk begins to move
between the little boat and everywhere,
and I'm too far out to hear the strum of breakers,
so I try to get the sense of something regular
and fix upon the beating light that's shoreward,
sure that I've left it not too far away.

.....Rod Jellema

You Are

My anchor my magnetic north
My coming home my setting forth
To my old craft the turning star
You are middle distance near and far
Lullaby sleep and reveille
My waking laughter ecstasy
My coming home and setting forth
My anchor and magnetic north

....Roland Flint

DNA

Like beads
      strung out in
            patient replication
                  adenine guanine
            cytosine   thymine
      guanine   cytosine
            adenine   thymine
                  cytosine....
                  4 character alpha
                  bet for mystic
                  WORD
                        evoking
                  hair eyes nails
            lungs intestines dreams
                  the myriad shapes of
                              cells
                  the forms of men
                        and with those men
            of gods, of worlds beyond
                  of means of speech
                  and codes beyond the code
                        beyond the
                        CODE

                              ....Frank Evans

171

Flying the Zuni Mountains
[excerpt]

This we know:
we are the wind.
We will come back gently over the lake,
we will lash the waves and bend the trees;
we will lie side by side on the high mountains
drinking martinis and telling the old jokes over.
Never our wings will melt or crumple with heat or hardness.
This we know.
For the man who draws the blueprints, shapes the wings,
    threads the bolts, pulls the props
is not our faith.
Ours is the wind and the wind is us
and no one shall bury us ever.

We have known space not surrounded by closets and
cabbages cooking,
we have whirled rainbows over our heads;
we have owned the earth by rising from it,
never again shall we walk with ordinary feet.

The wings were shaped from a woman's weeping...
no other tears shall fall.

....Ann Darr

On Duty

Gun-metal is somehow cool even in this heat.
They press the cherished barrels to their cheeks
From time to time. Little else is done,
Nothing said, except to blow down the neck
Of uniforms or peer into the sight of a rifle.

It sharpens a wavering landscape under the nose,
And capillaries of a browned, dust-caked leaf;
Including a man's lean, guarded figure, stepping clear
Of trees; whose bare soles seem to skip along
The steamy, bitumen-road, with hardly a touch.

It's a fragrance he loves, recalling days
When the giant Barber-Green unrolled its linoleum
Through the heart of this country.
It's a sight they have waited for all morning,
Beaten by this hottening monument hoisted now

To its zenith; rehearsing the features of this man,
Sure to come hot-stepping it to quench his thirst
At the official tap on the town's pipeline.
They have him lie face-down on the bonnet
Of a patrol car; its brand's warmth;

Its windscreen wipers poised on a dusty arc.
The engine's steady pulse drowns his own,
For it churrs and churrs, churning his memory
Like a broken record: how in broad daylight
They ordered three he knew to do press-ups

Till exhausted, then to run, barely able to break
Out of tottering before the guns blazed;
Giving his name as witness in the heat of it all,
And now this: a pistol to his head, they fire
An instruction, *Bwoy, we goin ge yu a chance, run!*

....Fred D'Aguiar

Baby Leopard

Every day I eat the zookeeper's food
Away from the grasslands of my rightful home,
Separated even from the zebra.

Every day the overwhelming tide of people
Swarm in from the gates.
They look at me and pass without a word.
Nobody cares what I think
under my green plastic canopy.

....Adam Chambers

Arithmetic

Once numbers were fun —
5 was orotund,
always holding forth to 6
who'd slide downhill,
rolling head over heels into 7
who'd stand ramrod straight,
not like that snaky 8,
even slipperier than 6
who'd do a backflip and turn
into 9 with its bulging top,
a tipsy lollipop, a ring
escaping its finger.

Now we're into subtraction,
that reckoning of loss.
I see a child who lets go
of a balloon and watches it fly
out of reach, past trees
and into the sky. His mouth

opens in a perfect O of disbelief,
and out come all the vowels of grief.

.....Nan Fry

When you read good literature, you realize the little modest steps people take, and the great bravery of people who were never even known.

....*Edgar Silex*

Writing memoir – or more precisely, creative non-fiction about my life – I hold my life in my hand like a fortune-teller's crystal ball. But instead of staring into the misty depth of the future, I turn this life to see my present self reflected in the past. My questions curve memories, moments, incidents into a new perspective so that I can see something I've never seen before.

....*Minnie Bruce Pratt*

Broken Wing

It was in front of the house where I grew up,
at the base of the big tree, a brown baby bird.
Not even 8 year old curiosity could find its mother.
So carefully, I stepped toward it,
watched its small, unmoving feathers,
its dark, unblinking eyes. After a few silent minutes
I scooped it up
gently. It was all heart
pounding against the cup of my palm.
Years later my parents abandoned the house,
married other people. The tree still stands
and I remember the moment, the bird's heart
pounding in my palm, its dark eyes
constant, looking for what is lost.

.... *Virginia Crawford*

Shapes, Vanishings

1

Down a street in the town where I went
to high school twenty-odd years ago, by doorways
and shadows that change with the times, I walked
past a woman at whose glance I almost stopped cold,
almost to speak, to remind her of who I had been—
but walked on, not being certain it was she,
not knowing what I might find to say.
It wasn't quite the face I remembered, the years
being what they are, and I could have been wrong.

2

But that feeling of being stopped cold, stopped dead,
will not leave me, and I hark back
to the thing I remember her for, though God knows
how I could remind her of it now.
Well, one afternoon when I was fifteen
I sat in her class. She leaned on her desk,
facing us, the blackboard behind her arrayed
with geometrical figures – triangle, square,
pentagon, hexagon, et cetera. She pointed
and named them. "The five-sided figure," she said,
"is a polygon." So far so good, but then when she said,
"The six-sided one is a hexagon," I wanted things clear.
Three or more sides is *poly*, I knew, but five only
is *penta*, and said so; she denied it,
and I pressed the issue, I, with no grades
to speak of, a miserable average to stand on
with an Archimedean pole – no world to move,
either, just a fact to get straight, but she
would have none of it, saying at last, "Are you
contradicting me?"

3

A small thing to remember a teacher for. Since then,
I have thought about justice often enough
to have earned my uncertainty about what it is,
but one hard fact from that day has stayed with me:
If you're going to be a smartass, you have to be right,
and not just some of the time. "Are you
contradicting me?" she had said, and I stopped
breathing a moment, the burden of her words
pressing down through me hard and quick, the huge
weight of knowing I was right, and beaten. She
had me. "No, ma'am," I managed to say, wishing
I had the whole thing down on tape to play back
to the principal, wishing I were ten feet tall
and never mistaken, ever, about anything in this world,
wishing I were older, and long gone from there.

4

Now I am older, and long gone from there.
What sense is a grudge over something so small?
What use to forgive her for something
she wouldn't remember? Now students
face me as I stand at my desk, and the shoe
may yet find its way to the other foot,
if it hasn't already. I couldn't charge
thirty-five cents for all that I know
of geometry; what little I learned is gone now,
like a face looming up for a second out of years
that dissolve in the mind like a single summer.
Therefore,
if ever she almost stops me again,
I will walk on as I have done once already,
remembering how we failed each other,
knowing better than to blame anyone.

.....*Henry Taylor*

I Took My Cousin to Prettyboy Dam

I took my cousin to Prettyboy Dam.
A boxer was swimming for sticks, the ripples
Blew from the left, and beer cans glittered
Under the poison-ivy.

We talked of pelota; and how the tendrils of vines
Curl opposite ways in the opposite hemispheres.
My cousin was dying.   By this I mean
The rate of his disengagement was rapid.

There was a haze of heat, and August boys
Chunked rocks at a bottle that bobbed on the water.
The slow hours enclosed the flight of instants,
Melted the picnic-ice.

Everything he saw differently, and more clearly than I.
The joined dragonflies, the solid foam of the fall;
The thin haste of the ant at my foot,
And me, as I looked at him.

We were close beside each other, speaking of
Pelota, chaining cigarettes when the matches were gone.
But we saw different things, since one could not say
"Wait...."
Nor the other "Come...."

...Josephine Jacobsen

A Poem For My Father

It could only have been you
Who lifted me to the high, thick branches
Strong enough to hold my weight

The cherry tree all in bloom,
A white ship on a green sea
Tacking north

And there among the murmur of bees' wings
I climbed through a cloud of blossom and

into the white heart of spring

....Michael Fallon

Horse Girls

1.

The only year I want a pony for Christmas,
my mother is crying, she asks me
for permission to leave.

I picture her for a moment, lifted up to sit behind a cowboy,
astride and waving, laughing even,
but I do not let her go.

She saddles me daily, in silence and rides me to school,
with her own careful stitching in the tackle.
The bridle reminds me to be pleasant.
She bits herself up to smile at the ladies in the
grocery store, though she talks to none of them.

and she stays and stays and stays

2.

Near the Grand Canyon, my forehead on the glass of the car window,
my chin on the blue vinyl of my parents' car, riding west.
I see you. All of you moves:
your tail is actually whipping, your mane is honestly shaking
and you are genuinely the black of agate.
You are the only wild thing I have ever seen.
I watch for as long as I can see you.

3.

When I played at her house,
she owned plastic horses,
our hands rode them
over the fields of clean wall to wall
while her mother vacuumed.

Inside my room,
I wished for carpeting
and long hair like hers.
I didn't wish for long though.

I could see, even then,
the fence posts my mother was digging holes for,
the turn of her pliers barbing the wire,

the thing she was grooming me to be.

....Maggie Polizos

Fledgling

Mother-may-I is not a game my son can play this fall.
Without permission, he strides toward endings, takes giant steps.
Can he be this slender man turning to me the clear eyes of my child?
The car crests the last, long ridge of hills and we sweep
down into the mountain valley he will soon think of as home.
He does not see a woman, stricken as Demeter, who knows how barren earth

will be this winter. He only looks to share his joy in country earth,
pungent with wood smoke and cider apples, smoldering with fall.
We jolt a rutted lane where honeysuckle thickets are the home
of startled quail. A peevish groundhog waddles down the steps
a sagging porch dips gingerly in the deep grass, as we sweep
up to a sun blistered frame house. "Needs some paint," says my child.

He waits my wan smile, then enter 'man of action' exit 'child',
lopes to a tire sprouting frost black tomatoes, pokes the earth
to find the key. I am ushered in with a deep bow, the sweep
of plumes. He glowers as he watches my face fall
at the blotches of mildew on the walls, cobweb festooned steps,
a sofa belching stuffing where field mice found a home.

Above the mantle, wreathed in flowers, 'Home Sweet Home',
cardboard stained behind splintered glass. It shall be for my child
I vow, grab mop and bucket to hurry up the steps.
I wipe the grime from windows, dreaming how soft this valley earth
will grow with apple bloom next spring. House cleaning spring and fall —
my mother battled soot and tarnish. "And we'll sweep

the cobwebs out of the sky," I hear her croon while I sweep
dried raisin flies from the larder in the home
of a goodwife spider. The toothpick bones of mice fall
onto my dust pan from a closet shelf. I wonder, will my child
remember, when I, too, am gone from earth,
his mother, kerchief askew, resting on these steps?

My son carries an armload of fire wood up the steps.
I rise to stand beside him, lift a hand to sweep
his cowlick flat, laugh at his astonished, "How on earth – "
He stares at scrubbed pine floors, the sunlit windows of his home,
then crunches me in the convulsive hug of a child.
I relish his transparent happiness. I will not let one tear fall.

We sit, shoulders touching, on the steps of his new home.
To the star sweep I say a silent, "*Vale Valeque*, child
of earth," for a moment grasp a God who lets sparrows fall.

....Marta Knobloch

On Assateague Island

we sipped
the late night
skinny
down
along
the open
coast
and wet
laid back
the stars
unzipped
the old
green tent
and then
there were
wild horses

....Charles Rossiter

I Don't Want to Grow Up

I don't want to grow up
because grownups have to do
too much work. Every day
they have to go to work, clean the house,
fix the food, and change the baby's pampers
when he stinks!

I'd rather be a kid
because when you're a kid you get lots of toys
and get to go outside and climb trees,
and ride a bike, and you don't have to go get food
and you don't have to call people names
or check the mail for bills.

....Dewitt Clinton

Taboo

I take into silence my silence – what
I will not say,
Watching white leaves in sunlight wave.
I tell myself,
I forgot what I would say. And birds
Flit by; their dark
Flashes dart along the old imprinting.
Green odors
Wake and turn. If I approach those wishes,
They talk back
From hiding places – worms emerging
After rain –
And so I sleep, afraid, small again, as I
Would be outside.
Sleep protects the way a window tells you
What to see:
The leaves, more yellow in the moving light.
Sleep tucks sound
Away. "Don't frown when you think,"
My mother said.
She came in with laundry. "Don't frown.
You'll wrinkle your skin."
Sleep helps in simple erasures, though what if
I remember
When the rain stopped and children played
Near rhododendron;
Oklahoma. Honeysuckle
Reached the windows,
And when my father watered vines, honey rinsed
The air again.
Perhaps it was then that I became silent
With my father.
I was six and watched from the porch as he

Let the water
Fall over petals and into the little straws
I always slipped
Out, touching honey on my tongue. He smiled
At me, but words –
What word first? And even now, when my father
Holds me, though he
Ages into white and blue, even now, well –
He whispers over
The tablecloth as Mother stacks
Dishes in the kitchen.
"You are like me," he says. "You dream."
Then Mother enters,
Balancing plates and forks, the leftover cake, what
The neighbors say.
"Did you notice the new fence? The birds did."
My father nods.
He looks at me. Through the window, birds call out,
In danger or mating.
If I knew what I heard, I would know what to say.

....Judith Hall

blessing the boats

at St. Mary's

may the tide
that is entering even now
the lip of our understanding
carry you out
beyond the face of fear
may you kiss
the wind then turn from it
certain that it will
love your back   may you
open your eyes to water
water waving forever
and may you in your innocence
sail through this to that

....Lucille Clifton

Susan in the Potter's Field

1.
If they went down far enough
they would tap into sweet water

but first they will have to spade
through cow pies, graves
of the cicada and what's left

of ferns, along with
two good used
clavicles,

cache of broken crockery

escape hatch of meadow
vole, the shrew's
asylum

mine

2.
Yesterday eight brawny men with straps
let you down that shaft

left you lying down there
with your blue dress
one cyclamen bloom and the skate key
a sister remembered you might need

Did you hear them muttering
about the dumb weight
before they let fall
the lid

The dark worried you, and the quiet
because it was always night when
the voices who got by without bodies
came

You're safe now —
even if they'd stowed away they can't
have skates on. And you came in first at this
once and remember better than
anyone in the family
the jingles.

It should be smooth going
down there you won't find sidewalks
with cracks, so if something breaks
in our mother

no one could blame you

3.
If they had gone down far enough
they could have reached sweet water —

the flower will go first
then your body
your blue gown

and last, the scuffed nickel of the key
will fall slowly through arch
of sternum to lie against the white column
of spine

and the lead box itself will fall slowly
a lift going down through many strata
of lives.
                You will be there before any of us.

But watch for us. Remember the way for us.
Help us get through
these verses in our right voice.

Help us with   tightening and loosening. A key

hangs by its string, banging against our chest
and we jerk along, hardly staying up.

....*Sarah Cotterill*

What I Am Waiting For

To linger longest; to be
still and quiet and good enough,
so that, one by one, the lights will flicker
and go out, at last, in that house: doors
rusted and slipped from their hinges, the old porch
giving way to rain, old angers falling away to silence;

I'll approach it then, the rough-
hewn house of my childhood, emptied,
dark, shutters banging in the wind;
I'll place my hand on the bannister,
and slowly climb, unpunished,
up the groaning stairs to a room that was mine;

I'll lie down on the bed and watch
the stars come out again
through that one small window
where the safe world once glistened
and shone beyond me like the God I prayed to
who did not save me from anything;

Maybe then the knots in me
will come undone; maybe I will
be so whole for once I'll sleep all night
though the owls screech in the moony trees
and the weasels call out to each other again and again
far off in the complicated dark.

....Anne Caston

Evening Marshes

Marsh grass is golden
Under a late sun,
And wild ducks' wings
Whistle with the wind.
We are one,
Wild duck and setting sun,
Marsh grass around the pond,
Earth smells and shadows,
Coming cold and early night,
Evening star and this
Great emptiness
Within me.

....*Gilbert Byron*

Shouts of Holy Welcome

When it comes down to this,
when it comes down to branches
and the dry bits of sky stuck between,
down to a belief in foliage
but not a leaf to show –
no tracing even,
the stems that let go
on a single afternoon:

when it comes down to earth,
which is what
everything comes down to,
and to memory
and to failing memory,
failing or confused
or flatter in detail
or smaller in consequence

and you are less
than anyone you see
out on the street
busy with packages,
eager or almost eager
or at least untroubled,
the wide bargain
of your own intelligence

narrowed to attention
(threads picked from the rug,
prints rubbed from the mirror),
attention that surveys
room after room
with no plan,
hoping to be stopped for supper,
for whatever comes next,

someone else's choice –
your own will
lost with names of planets,
nightsounds, things you knew
when you knew
that even though
every kind of damage has been done
somewhere to someone,

beauty stays:
beauty thrashing in you,
the sad beautiful limbs
unencumbered and willing,
the evening walk from work,
the children waiting
just behind the one door
you will always reach to open,

even now,
having heard
all there is to hear
in your favor
numb and in terror,
patronized by love –
a patient whose treatment
does not work –

reach to turn the brass knob
and turn it,
the voices starting up
inside for you,
the leaps
down stairs,
the shouts
of holy welcome.

...Judy Bolz

You Wear Cowboy Hats and Drive Fast

He said.

You wear spurs when the moon is high
and drink the night away.

He said.

You love smoke, rocky cliffs,
and guitars out of tune.

He said.

You think you're
Geronimo/Greer Garson/Annie Oakley/Jeff Chandler.

He said.

You own the last Detroit convertible
in the county and there isn't a trucker around
you won't play.

He said.

Sky King don't have nothing on you –
You, with your cowboy hat, baying at the moon,
Driving fast for tomorrow.

...*Jessica Frances Locklear*

The story tells you about the teller as much as it tells you about the truth of the story.

....Wayne Karlin

The Tragedy of Hats

is that you can never see the one you're wearing,
that no one believes the lies they tell,
that they grow to be more famous than you,
that you could die in one but you won't be buried in it.

That we use them to create dogs
in our own image. That the dogs
in their mortarboards and baseball caps and veils
crush our hubris with their unconcern.

That Norma Desmond's flirty cocktail hat flung aside
left a cowlick that doomed her. That two old ladies
catfighting in Hutzler's Better Dresses both wore flowered
straw. Of my grandmother the amateur hatmaker:

this legend: that the holdup man at the Mercantile
turned to say Madam I love your hat before
he shot the teller dead who'd giggled at her
homemade velvet roses. O happy tragedy of hats!

That they make us mimic classic gestures,
inspiring pleasure first, then pity and then fear.
See how we tip them, hold them prettily against the wind
or pull them off and mop our sweaty brows

like our beloved foolish dead in photographs.
Like farmers plowing under the ancient sun.

....Clarinda Harriss

Poem for My Sons

When you were born, all the poets I knew
were men, dads eloquent on their sleeping
babes and the future: Coleridge at midnight,
Yeats' prayer that his daughter lack opinions,
his son be high and mighty, think and act.
You've read the new father's loud eloquence,
fiery sparks written in a silent house
breathing with the mother's exhausted sleep.

When you were born, my first, what I thought was
milk: my breasts sore, engorged, but not enough
when you woke. With you, my youngest, I did not
think: my head unraised for three days, mind-dead
from waist-down anesthetic labor, saddle
block, no walking either.
                              Your father was then
the poet I'd ceased to be when I got married.
It's taken me years to write this to you.

I had to make a future, willful, voluble,
lascivious, a thinker, a long walker,
unstruck transgressor, furious, shouting,
voluptuous, a lover, a smeller of blood,
milk, a woman mean as she can be some nights,
existence I could pray to, capable of
poetry.
          Now here we are. You are men,
and I am not the woman who rocked you
in the sweet reek of penicillin, sour milk,
the girl who could not imagine herself
or a future more than a warm walled room,
had no words but the pap of the expected,
and so, those nights, could not wish for you.

But now I have spoken, my self, I can ask
for you: that you'll know evil when you smell it;
that you'll know good and do it, and see how both
run loose through your lives; that then you'll remember
you come from dirt and history; that you'll choose
memory, not anesthesia; that you'll have work
you love, hindering no one, a path crossing
at boundary markers where you question power;
that your loves will match you thought for thought
in the long heat of blood and fact of bone.

Words not so romantic nor so grandly tossed
as if I'd summoned the universe to be
at your disposal.
                    I can only pray:

That you'll never ask for the weather, earth,
angels, women, or other lives to obey you;

that you'll remember me, who crossed, recrossed
you,
            as a woman making slowly toward
an unknown place where you could be with me,
like a woman on foot, in a long stepping out.

                                ....Minnie Bruce Pratt

Tears

"Save us from tears that bring no healing..."
Matthew Arnold

When the ophthalmologist told me gravely
that I didn't produce enough tears,
I wanted to say: but I cry too much
and too often. At airports and weddings
and sunsets. At bad movies

where the swell of sentimental music
forces open my tear ducts
like so many locks in a canal.
And when he handed me this vial
of artificial tears, I wanted to tell him

about Niobe. Perhaps if her tear ducts
had been deficient, she wouldn't
have dissolved into salty water
after the loss of her children.
Maybe other heroes and heroines

deprived of the resonant ability to cry
would have picked themselves up
and acted sensibly. Othello for instance
weeping, before he killed her,
into Desdomona's embroidered pillow.

And so I take this bottle of distilled grief
and put it in the back of a drawer,
but I don't throw it away. There may be poems
in my future that need to be watered,
for I still remember Tennyson

who wrote of how short swallow-flights of song
dip their wings in tears, and skim away.

....Linda Pastan

Vietnam is a black and white photograph of my grandparents sitting in bamboo chairs in their front courtyard. They are sitting tall and proud, surrounded by chickens and roosters. Their feet are separated from the dirt by thin sandals. My grandfather's broad forehead is shining. So too are my grandmother's famed sad eyes. The animals are obliviously pecking at the ground. This looks like a wedding portrait though it is actually a photograph my grandparents had taken late in life, for their children, especially for my mother. When I think of this portrait of my grandparents in the last years of their life, I always envision a beginning. To what or where, I don't know, but always a beginning.

When my mother, a Catholic school girl from the South, decided to marry my father, a Buddhist gangster from the North, her parents disowned her. This is in the photograph, though it is not visible to the eye. If it were, it would be a deep impression across the soft dirt of my grandparents' courtyard. Her father chased her out of the house, beating her with the same broom she had used every day of her life, from the time she could stand up and sweep to the morning of the very day she was chased away.

The year my mother met my father, there were several young men working at her house, running errands for her father, pickling vegetables with her mother. It was understood by everyone that these men were courting my mother. My mother claims she had no such understanding.

She treated these men as brothers, sometimes as uncles even, later exclaiming in self-defense: I didn't even know about love then.

Ma says love came to her in a dark movie theater. She doesn't remember what movie it was or why she'd gone to see it, only that she'd gone alone and found herself sitting beside him. In the dark, she couldn't make out his face but noticed he was handsome. She wondered if he knew she was watching him out of the corner of her eye. Watching him without embarrassment or shame. Watching him with a strange curiosity, a feeling which made her want to trace and retrace his silhouette with her fingertips until she'd memorized every feature and could call his face to her in any dark place she passed through. Later, in the shadow of the beached fishing boats on the blackest nights of the year, she would call him to mind, his face a warm companion for her body on the edge of the sea.

In the early days of my parents' courtship, my mother told stories. She confessed elaborate dreams about the end of war: foods she'd eat (a banquet table, mangos piled high to the ceiling); songs she'd make up and sing, clapping her hands over her head and throwing her hair like a horse's mane; dances she'd do, hopping from one foot to the other. Unlike the responsible favorite daughter or sister she was to her family, with my father, in the forest, my mother became reckless, drunk on her youth and the possibility of love. Ignoring the chores to be done at home, she rolled her pants up to her knees, stuck her bare feet in puddles, and learned to smoke a cigarette.

She tied a vermilion ribbon in her hair. She became moody. She did her chores as though they were favors to her family, forgetting that she ate the same rice, and was dependent on the same supply of food. It seemed to her the face which stared back at her from deep inside the family well was the face of a woman she had never seen before. At night she lay in bed and thought of his hands, the way his thumb flicked down on the lighter and brought fire to her cigarette. She began to wonder what the forests were like before the trees were dying. She remembered her father had once described to her the smiling broadness of leaves, jungles-thick in the tangle of rich soil.

One evening, she followed my father in circles through the forest, supposedly in search of the clearing which would take them to his aunt's house. They wandered aimlessly into darkness, never finding the clearing or the aunt she knew he never had.

"You're not from here," she said.

"I know."

"So tell me, what's your aunt's name?"

"Xuan."

"Spring?"

"Yes."

She laughed. I can't be here, she thought.

"My father will be looking for me"—

"I'll walk you home. It's not too late."

In the dark, she could feel his hand extending toward her, filling the space between them. They had not touched once the entire evening and now he stood offering his hand to her. She stared at him for a long time. There was a small scar on his chin, curved like her fingernail. It was too dark to see this. She realized she had memorized his face.

My first memory of my father's face is framed by the coiling barbed wire of a prison camp in South Vietnam. My mother's voice crosses through the wire. She is whispering his name and in this utterance, caressing him. Over and over, she calls him to her, "Anh Minh, Anh Minh." His name becomes a tree she presses her body against. The act of calling blows around them like a warm breeze and when she utters her own name, it is the second half of a verse which began with his. She drops her name like a pebble is dropped into a well. She wants to be engulfed by him, "Anh Minh, em My. Anh Minh. Em, em My."

She is crossing through barbed wire the way some people step through open windows. She arrives warm, the slightest film of sweat on her bare arms. She says, "It's me, it's me." Shy and formal and breathless, my parents are always meeting for the first time. Savoring the sound of a name, marveling at the bone structure.

I trail behind them, the tip of their dragon's tail. I am suspended like a silk banner from the body of a kite. They flick me here and there. I twist and turn in the air, connected to them by this fabric which worms spin.

For a handful of pebbles and my father's sharp profile my mother left home and never returned. Imagine a handful of pebbles. The casual way he tossed them at her as she was walking home from school with her girlfriends. He did this because he liked her and wanted to let her know. Boys are dumb that way, my mother told me. A handful of pebbles, to be thrown in anger, in desperation, in joy. My father threw them in love. Ma says they touched her like warm kisses, these pebbles which he had been holding in the sun. Warm kisses on the curve of her back, sliding down the crook of her arm, grazing her ankles and landing around her feet in the hot sand.

What my father told her could have been a story. There was no one in the South to confirm the details of his life. He said he came from a semi-aristocratic Northern family. Unlacing his boot, he pulled out his foot and told her to pay close attention to how his second toe was significantly longer than his other toes. "A sure sign of aristocracy," he claimed. His nose was high, he said, because his mother was French, one of the many mistresses his father kept. He found this out when he was sixteen. That year he ran away from home and came south.

"There are thieves, gamblers, drunks I've met who remind me of people in my family. It's the way they're dreamers. My family's a garden full of dreamers lying on their backs, staring at the sky, drunk and choking on their dreaming." He said this while leaning against a tree, his arms folded across his bare chest, his eyes staring at the ground, his shoulders golden.

She asked her mother, "What does it mean if your second toe is longer than your other toes?"

"It means....your mother will die before your father," her mother said.

"I heard somewhere it's a sign of aristocracy."

"Huh! What do we know about aristocracy?"

My father's toes fascinated my mother. When she looked at his bare feet she saw ten fishing boats, two groups of five. Within each group, the second boat ventured ahead, leading the others. She would climb a tree, stand gripping the branch with her own toes and stare down at his. She directed him to stand in the mud. There, she imagined what she saw to be ten small boats surrounded by black water, a fleet of junks journeying in the dark.

She would lean back and enjoy this vision, never explaining to him what it was she saw. She left him to wonder about her senses as he stood, cigarette in hand, staring at her trembling ankles, not moving until she told him to.

I was born in the alley behind my grandparents' house. At three in the morning my mother dragged herself out of the bed in the small house she and my father lived in after they married.

He was in prison, so alone, she began to walk. She cut a crooked line on the beach. Moving in jerky steps, like a ball tossed on the waves, she seemed to be thrown along without direction. She walked to the schoolhouse, sat on the sand and leaned against the first step. She felt grains of sand pressing against her back. Each grain was a minute pin prick which became increasingly painful to her. She felt as though her back would break out in a wash of blood. She thought, I am going to bleed to death. We are going to die.

In front of the schoolhouse lay a long metal tube. No one knew where it came from. It seemed always to have been there. Children hid in it, crawled through it, spoke to one another at either ends of it, marched across it, sat on it and confided secrets beside it. There had been so little to play with at the school recesses. This long metal tube became everything. A tarp was suspended over it, to shield it from the sun. The tube looked like a blackened log which sat in a room without walls. When the children sat in a line on the tube, their heads bobbing this way and that in conversation, it seemed they were sitting under a canopied raft.

The night I was born, my mother looked at this tube and imagined it to be the badly burnt arm of a dying giant whose body was buried in the sand. She could not decide if he had been buried in the sand and was trying to get out or if he had tried to bury himself in the sand but was unable to pull his arm under in time. In time for what? She had heard a story about a girl in a neighboring town who was killed during a napalm bombing. The bombing happened on an especially hot night, when this girl had walked to the beach to cool her feet in the water. They found her floating on the sea. The phosphorous from the napalm made her body glow like a lantern. In her mind, my mother built a canopy for this girl. She started to cry, thinking of the buried giant, the floating girl, these bodies stopped in mid-step, on their way somewhere.

She began to walk toward the tube. She had a sudden urge to be inside of it. The world felt dangerous to her and she was alone. At the mouth of the tube, she bent down, her belly blocked the opening. She tried the other side, the other mouth. Again, her belly stopped her. "But I remember," she muttered out loud, "as a girl I sometimes slept in here." This was what she wanted now, to sleep inside the tube.

"Tall noses come from somewhere– "
"Not from here."
"Not tall noses."

Eyes insinuate, moving from her nose to mine then back again. Mouths suck air in, form it into the darkest shade of contempt, then spit it at her feet as she walks by. I am riding on her hip. I am the new branch that makes the tree bend but she walks with her head held high. She knows where she pulled me from. No blue eye.

Ma says war is a bird with a broken wing flying over the countryside, trailing blood and burying crops in sorrow. If something grows in spite of this it is both a curse and a miracle. When I was born, she cried when I cried, knowing I had breathed war in and she could never shake it out of me. Ma says war makes it dangerous to breathe though she knows you die if you don't. She says she could have thrown me against the wall, breaking me until I coughed up this war which is killing us all. She could have stomped on it in the dark, and danced on it like a mad woman dancing on grave stones. She could have ground it down to powder and spit on it but didn't I know? War has no beginning and no end. It crosses oceans like a splintered boat filled with people singing a sad song.

Every morning Ahn wakes up in the house next to mine, a yellow duplex she and I call a townhouse because we found out from a real estate ad that a townhouse is a house that has an upstairs and a downstairs. My father calls Ahn the chicken egg girl. Each morning Ahn's mother loads a small push cart with stacks of eggs and Ahn walks all over Linda Vista selling eggs. Her backyard is full of chickens and roosters. Sometimes you can see a rooster fly up and balance itself on the back gate and it will crow and crow, off and on, all day long, until dark comes.

We live in the country of California, the province of San Diego, the village of Linda Vista. We live in old Navy Housing bungalows which were built in the 1940's and 50's. Since the 1980's, these bungalows house Vietnamese, Cambodian, and Laotian refugees from the Vietnam War. When we moved in, we had to sign a form promising not to put fishbones down the garbage disposal.

We live in a yellow house on Westinghouse Street. Our house is one story, made of wood and plaster. We are connected to six two-story houses and another one-story house at the other end. Across from our row of houses, separated by a field of brown dirt, sits another row of yellow houses, same as ours, and facing us like a sad twin. Linda Vista is full of houses like ours, painted in peeling shades of olive green, baby blue, and sun-baked yellow.

There's new Navy Housing on Linda Vista Road, the long street that takes you out of here. We see them watering their lawns, the children riding pink tricycles up and down the *cul-de-sacs*. We see them in Victory Supermarket, buying groceries with cash. In Kelley Park they have picnics and shoot each other with water guns. At school, their kids are Most Popular, Most Beautiful, Most Likely to Succeed. Though there are more Vietnamese, Cambodian, and Laotian kids at the school, we are not the most of anything in the yearbook. They call us Yang because one year a bunch of Laotian kids with the last name Yang came to our school. The Navy Housing kids started calling all the refugee kids Yang.

Yang. Yang. Yang.

Ma says living next to Ahn's family reminds her of Vietnam because the blue tarp suspended above Ahn's backyard is the bright blue of the South China Sea.

Ma says isn't it funny how sky and sea follow you from place to place as if they too were traveling and not just the boat that travels across or between them. Ma says even Ahn reminds her of Vietnam, the way she sets out for market each morning.

Ba becomes a gardener. Overnight. He buys a truck full of equipment and a box of business cards from Uncle Twelve, who is moving to Texas to become a fisherman. The business cards read: Tom's Professional Gardening Service, and have a small, green embossed picture of a man pushing a lawn mower. The man's back is to the viewer, so no one who doesn't already know can tell it's not Ba. He says I can be his secretary because I speak the best English. If you call us on the business phone, you will hear me say: "Hello, you have reached Tom's professional gardening service. We are not here right now but if you leave us a message, we will get back to you as soon as possible. Thank you."

It is hot and dusty where we live. Some people think it's dirty but they don't know much about us. They haven't seen our gardens full of lemongrass, mint, cilantro, and basil. They've only seen the pigeons pecking at day-old rice and the skinny cats and dogs sitting in the skinny shade of skinny trees, as they drive by. Have they seen the berries we pick which turn our lips and fingertips red? How about the small staircase Ba built from our bedroom window to the backyard so I would have a shortcut to the clothesline? How about the Great Wall of China which snakes like a river, from the top of the steep Crandall Street hill to the slightly curving bottom? Who has seen this?

It was so different at the Green Apartment. We had to close the gate behind us every time we came in. It clanged heavily, and I imagined a host of eyes, upstairs and downstairs, staring at me from behind slightly parted curtains. There were four palm trees planted at the four far corners of the courtyard and a central staircase which was narrow at the top and fanned out at the bottom. The steps were covered in fake grass, like the set of an old Hollywood movie, the kind that stars an aging beauty who wakes up to find something is terribly wrong.

We moved out of the Green Apartment when we turned on the TV one night and heard that our manager and his brother had hacked a woman to pieces and dumped her body into the Pacific Ocean in ten-gallon garbage bags which washed onto the shore. Ma said she didn't want to live in a place haunted by a murdered lady. So we moved to Linda Vista where she said there were a lot of Vietnamese people like us, people whose only sin is a little bit of gambling and sucking on fish bones and laughing hard and arguing loudly.

Ma shaved all her hair off in Linda Vista because she got mad at Ba for gambling her money away and getting drunk every week watching Monday Night Football. Ba gave her a blue baseball cap to wear until her hair grew back and she wore it backwards, like a real bad-ass.

After that, some people in Linda Vista said that Ma was crazy and Ba was crazy for staying with her. But what do some people know?

When the photograph came, Ma and Ba got into a fight. Ba threw the fish tank out the front door and Ma broke all the dishes. They said they never should've been together.

Ma's sister sent her the photograph from Vietnam. It came in a stiff envelope. There was nothing inside but the photograph, as if anything more would be pointless. Ma started to cry. "Child," she sobbed, over and over again. She wasn't talking about me. She was talking about herself.

Ba said, "Don't cry. Your parents have forgiven you."

Ma kept crying anyway and told him not to touch her with his gangster hands. Ba clenched his hands into tight fists and punched the walls.

"What hands?! What hands?!" he yelled. "Let me see the gangster! Let me see his hands!" I see his hands punch hands punch hands punch blood.

Ma is in the kitchen. She has torn the screen off the window. She is punctuating the pavement with dishes, plates, cups, rice bowls. She sends them out like birds gliding through the sky with nowhere in particular to go. Until they crash. Then she exhales, "Huh!" in satisfaction.

I am in the hallway gulping air. I breathe in the breaking and the bleeding. When Ba plunges his hands into the fish tank, I detect the subtle tint of blood in water. When he throws the fish tank out the front door, yelling, "Let me see the gangster!" I am drinking up spilled water and swallowing whole the beautiful colored tropical fishes before they hit the ground, caking themselves in brown dirt until just the whites of their eyes remain, blinking at the sun.

All the hands are in my throat, cutting themselves on broken dishes and the fish swim in circles, they can't see for all the blood.

Ba jumps in his truck and drives away.

When I grow up I am going to be the gangster we are all looking for.

The neighborhood kids are standing outside our house, staring in through the windows and the open door. Even Ahn, our chicken egg seller. I'm sure their gossiping mothers sent them to spy on us. I run out front and dance like a crazy lady, dance like a fish, wiggle my head and throw my body so everything eyes nose tongue comes undone. At first they laugh but then they stop, not knowing what to think. Then I stop and stare each one of them down.

"What're you looking at?" I ask.

"Lookin' at you," one boy says, half-giggling.

"Well," I say, with my hand on my hip and my head cocked to one side, "I'm looking at you too,"and I give him my evil one-eye look, focusing all my energy into one eye. I stare at him hard like my eye is a bullet and he can be dead.

I turn my back on them and walk into the house.

I find Ma sitting in the window sill. The curve of her back is inside the bedroom while the rest of her body is outside, on the first step Ba built going from the bedroom to the garden. Without turning to look at me, she says, "Let me lift you into the attic."

"Why?"

"We have to move your grandparents in."

I don't really know what she is talking about but I say, "okay" anyway.

We have never needed the attic for anything. In fact, we have never gone up there. When we moved my grandparents in, Ma simply lifted me up and I pushed the attic door open with one hand while with the other, I slipped in the stiff envelope containing the photograph of my grandparents. I pushed it the length of my arm and down to my fingertips. I pushed it so far it was beyond reach but Ma said it was enough, they had come to live with us and sometimes you don't need to see or touch people to know they're there.

Ba came home drunk that night and asked to borrow my blanket. I heard him climbing the tree in the backyard. It took him a long time. He kept missing the wooden blocks which run up and down the tree like a ladder. Ba put them in when he built the steps going from the bedroom window into the garden. If you stand on the very top block, your whole body is hidden by tree branches. Ba put those blocks in for me, so I could win at hide-and-go-seek.

When Ba finally made it onto the roof, he lay down over my room and I could hear him rolling across my ceiling. Rolling and crying. I was scared he would roll off the edge and kill himself so I went to wake Ma.

She was already awake. She said it would be a good thing if he rolled off. But later, I heard someone climb the tree and all night two bodies rolled across my ceiling. Slowly and firmly they pressed against my sleep, the Catholic school girl and the Buddhist gangster, two dogs chasing each other's tails. They have been running like this for so long, they have become one dog one tail.

Without any hair and looking like a man, my mother is still my mother though sometimes I can't see her even when I look and look and look so long all the colors of the world begin to swim and bob around me. Her hands always bring me up, her big peasant hands with the flat, wide nails, wide like her nose and just as expressive. I will know her by her hands and her walk which is at once slow and urgent, the walk of a woman going to the market with her goods securely bound to her side. Even walking empty-handed, my mother suggests invisible bundles whose contents no one but she can unravel. And if I never see her again, I will know my mother by the smell of sea salt and the prints of my own bare feet crossing sand, running to and away from, to and away from, family.

When the eviction notice came, we didn't believe it so we threw it away. It said we had a month to get out. The houses on our block had a new owner who wanted to tear everything down and build better housing for the community. It said we were priority tenants for the new complex but we couldn't afford to pay the new rent so it didn't matter. The notice also said that if we didn't get out in time, all our possessions would be confiscated in accordance with some section of a law book or manual we were supposed to have known about but had never seen. We couldn't believe the eviction notice so we threw it away.

The fence is tall, silver, and see-through. Chain-link, it rattles when you shake it and wobbles when you lean against it. It circles the block like a bad dream. It is not funny like a line of laundry whose flying shirts and empty pants suggest human birds and vanishing acts. This fence presses sharply against your brain. We three stand still as posts. Looking at it, then at each other – this side and that – out of the corners of our eyes. What are we thinking?

At night we come back with three uncles. Ba cuts a hole in the fence and we step through. Quiet, we break into our own house through the back window. Quiet, we steal back everything that is ours. We fill ten-gallon garbage bags with clothes, pots and pans, flip-flops, the porcelain figure of Mary, and our wooden Buddha. In the arc of our flashlights we find our favorite hairbrushes behind bedposts. When we are done, we are clambering and breathless. We can hear police cars coming to get us though it's quiet.

We tumble out the window like people tumbling across continents. We are time traveling, weighed down by heavy furniture and bags of precious junk. We find ourselves leaning against Ba's yellow truck. Ma calls his name, her voice reaching like a hand feeling for a tree trunk in darkness.

In the car, Ma starts to cry. What about the sea, she asks. What about the garden? Ba says we can come back in the morning and dig up the stalks of lemongrass and fold the sea into a blue square. Ma is sobbing. She is beating the dashboard with her fists. "I want to know," she says, "I want to know, I want to know....who is doing this to us?" Hiccuping she says, "I want to know, why – why there's always a fence. Why there's always someone on the outside wanting someone.... something on the inside and between them....this....sharp-fence. Why are we always leaving like this?"

Everyone is quiet when Ma screams.

"Take me back!" she says. "I can't go with you. I've forgotten my mother and father. I can't believe....Anh Minh, we've left them to die. Take me back."

Ma wants Ba to stop the car but Ba doesn't know why. The three uncles, sitting in a line in the back of the truck, think Ma is crazy. They yell in through the window.

"My, are you going to walk back to Vietnam?"

"Yeah, are you going to walk home to your parents' house?"

In the silence another laughs.

Ba puts his foot on the gas pedal. Our car jerks forward, then plunges down the Crandall Street hill. Ma says, "I need air, water...." I roll the window down. She puts her head in her hands. She keeps crying. "Child." Outside, I see the Great Wall of China. In the glare of the street lamps, it is just a long strip of cardboard.

In the morning, the world is flat. Westinghouse Street is lying down like a jagged brush stroke of sun-burnt yellow. There is a big sign inside the fence that reads,

COMING SOON: Condominiums

Townhouses

Family Homes

Beside these words is a water color drawing of a large, pink complex.

We stand on the edge of the chain-link fence, sniffing the air for the scent of lemongrass, scanning this flat world for our blue sea. A wrecking ball dances madly through our house. Everything has burst wide open and sunk down low. Then I hear her calling them. She is whispering, "Ma/Ba, Ma/Ba." The whole world is two butterfly wings rubbing against my ear.

Listen....they are sitting in the attic, sitting like royalty. Shining in the dark, buried by a wrecking ball. Paper fragments floating across the surface of the sea.

Not a trace of blood anywhere except here, in my throat, where I am telling you all this.

....lê thi diem thúy

It's late afternoon on a hot Friday in early June, and I'm sitting in a plaza in a close-in suburb of Washington, D.C. I'm working, without much energy, on a typical summer project for an English professor: a study of the funeral elegies of Puritan New England. I always write my scholarship in public places like this. Writing is lonely work even when your subject isn't seventeenth-century funerary poems, and it's a comfort to look up and see people going about their business.

A swing band is setting up for the weekly dance here in Bethesda Square. The musicians are adjusting their music stands, donning their outfits – huge Hawaiian shirts – and warming up. They have a familiar look about them, a hip goofiness: big guys with beatnik goatees and little guys with thick glasses, nearly all with anachronistic American Bandstand hair. In the midst of the beeps and honks and scales, I hear the drummer tuning his snare drum. I can't see him, but his tentative tapping tells me exactly what he's doing as he works his way around the rim, pausing to adjust a lug here and there with his drum key. From the rising pitch of the taps I can tell that he's "tuning up," tightening the drumhead and the snares stretched across the bottom. You do that when you're playing with a big group and you want the drum crisp enough to cut through a lot of noise. If this were a small combo he'd be "tuning down," loosening the head and snares for a mushier sound.

By now a crowd has gathered, and the leader kicks things off with a bouncy rendition of "In the Mood." I collect my papers and wander over to watch the drummer. He is about my age, mid-forties, with thinning sandy hair. He might be new to this band; he's keeping his eyes glued to the charts. New or not, he's a real pro. He has a light foot on the bass drum and his hi-hat is as regular as a clock. His accents on the snare are right where they should be, punching up the section work from the brass. He's long since learned the secret to driving a big band: rushing the beat slightly. A good drummer constantly fights entropy. Most musicians tend to drag the beat, and a sluggish, lead-footed drummer only makes things worse.

This is tasteful, workmanlike drumming, the kind you *feel* more than hear, and at the band's first break I consider going up and telling him how good he is. In the end I decide against it. After all, he's just doing his job, and besides, I've always known that my appreciation of good drumming is borderline obsessive. What if I started babbling, unable to conceal a degree of enthusiasm that middle-aged guys are supposed to have outgrown? And what if the conversation took its inevitable turn and he asked, "Do you play?" I could say "I used to," but that response would leave so much untold that it would feel like a lie.

There's a joke that high school band directors tell, and it goes like this: God created the world in three days. On the first day He created singers, and He said that it was good. On the second He created musicians, and He said that it was good. On the third He created drummers, and He said, "Two out of three ain't bad." I heard that joke a lot when I was in high school, always with a twinge of self-righteous indignation. After all, *I* was a drummer.

Until ninth grade I hadn't been much of anything except what grownups called "a nice young man," the kind who got paid for babysitting other kids only a year or two younger than I was. Parents were always pleased when I hung out with their sons because they figured there would be no trouble. Naturally, I was embarrassed by this reputation, in part because it wasn't something I had set out to achieve. It seemed to me a pure product of my round, bland face. One look at me and you knew I wasn't about to down a six-pack of low Stroh's and urinate into your gas tank. Since grownups "knew" this, I figured I had no choice but to go along with it.

In ninth grade I decided to cultivate a cooler image, and began neglecting my homework and making wisecracks in class. But I couldn't manage to get myself into any real trouble: instead of getting mad, my teachers just got concerned. It seemed unfair. Scott Carlson could tell the civics teacher to kiss his royal ass and get sent to detention like a regular guy. Whenever I acted up, the teacher would call my parents in for a conference.

Mom and Dad were bewildered. How could their nice, bookish son be making Bs and Cs? James Dean was dead but not forgotten, and with all the talk about juvenile delinquency, they probably figured that midnight heroin runs to Cleveland were coming next. My father, an intuitive behaviorist, said he didn't give a damn *what* the problem was as long as I fixed it: "Shape up this summer or there's going to be world news made in this house." My mother, a committed believer in Dr. Spock, took me to an adolescent psychologist in Toledo, fifty miles away. I didn't pose much of a diagnostic challenge. The psychologist said I was acting up because I didn't have any interests that involved other people. The interests I did have — ancient Egypt, for instance — were all quirky, private things. Fifteen years later, I suppose, he would have said "get a life." He could work me into his schedule, but before my next session I had to come up with five school activities that I'd be willing to try.

It was sad watching Mom fumble with her checkbook as she paid for the session, and on the drive home I promised to get involved in school activities like a normal kid. Scrambling for something concrete, I remembered that my older brother, now in college, had been in the marching band. Wasn't some of his drum stuff – a pair of marching sticks, a rubber drum pad, some old lesson books –still in the closet of the room we had shared? If I started taking drum lessons, could we cancel next week's appointment?

My teacher was a jazz drummer named Bill Sims, who drove over from Lima on Thursday afternoons to give lessons in a soundproof booth at the back of Carter's Music Store. An immense black man in his early thirties, Bill had a goatee, an easy smile, and huge arms that made his hands look too small to be a drummer's hands. He was a passionate believer in solid foundations and meticulous technique. Don't get lazy: stick to the correct grip and turn those wrists until it hurts. No sloppy buzz rolls: keep those rolls clean and open, so you can hear every stroke. Learn to sight-read: don't play anything until you can count it out. Above all, get the fundamentals, which meant learning the twenty-six standard "rudiments" for the snare drum: the five-stroke roll, the flam-tap, the ratamacue, the paradiddle, and all the rest.

I learned quickly, working through Books I and II of *Haskell Harr's Method for Snare Drum* in six weeks. Then Bill started teaching me how to play a drum set, using a mock-up consisting of drum pads bolted together. He worked me through the basic rhythms: jazz, blues, swing, rock, country, polka, and Latin. Bill stressed "independence," the ability to play different rhythms simulta-neously. This purposeful devolution of the body's inclination toward symmetry was just weird enough to be fun. Learning to play straight eighth notes with one hand and triplets with the other felt like un-learning how to walk.

I rapped out my exercises on my brother's rubber Gladstone pad and a practice "set" assembled from coffee cans, tin pie-plates, and imaginary foot pedals. Before long I developed a drummer's hands, with leathery calluses and thickened muscles in the joint between thumb and forefinger. All the practice kept me from noticing something else I was acquiring: a drummer's heart. I discovered *that* one day in mid-August, after my lesson. I was Bill's last student of the day, and Carter's had already closed when we finished. Bill took me to the front of the empty store, sat me down at one of the new drum sets on display, and ran me through some of the standard rhythms I'd been learning. The tinks and clunks and thumps of the mock-drums I'd been practicing on had not prepared me for the depth and range of the sounds I was getting from these real drums, these shimmering red swirl Slingerlands with shiny chrome hoops and genuine Avedis Zildian cymbals.

Bill peeled the cellophane from a Count Basie album and placed the record carefully on the turntable of one of the display hi-fi's. Then he cranked up the volume and mouthed, "Swing it, man." Astonished to find that I actually could, I swung it, man, meshing with "Night Train" as the late afternoon sunlight streamed through the storefront window.

I left ninth grade and Donnell Junior High an amiable goof. When I entered tenth grade at Findlay Senior High I was an amiable goof who could play the drums. I joined every musical activity available: marching band, concert band, orchestra, swing band, pep band, pit bands for school musicals. That Christmas I got my own drums, a used set of Ludwigs that Bill found in the classifieds. The set was minimal but solid: a twenty-inch silver sparkle bass drum and one matching tom-tom, a high-hat with sixteen-inch cymbals, a single eighteen-inch ride cymbal, and a gleaming chrome-shell snare.

Drumming brought an immediate social payoff, especially after I joined a rock band and started playing at dances in the school cafeteria after football games and at the local teen center. I learned, to my amazement, that even barely competent three-chord rock bands playing sock-hops attracted groupies. I felt awkward when girls came up to talk to me after a dance, but it was a pleasant awkwardness for a change.

Now that I had a social identity I stopped acting up, to my parents' great relief. On a deeper level, though, the psychologist's plan to turn me into a more "normal" kid backfired. The fact was, drumming had simply become my newest obsession. I poured over textbooks on orchestral percussion, studying the proper techniques for tympani, tambourine, wood blocks, cymbals, and the deceptively simple triangle. Important percussive controversies emerged at every turn. Should a triangle be struck on its inside surface or on the outside? Should the fulcrum for a tympani roll be the thumb and forefinger or the thumb and second finger? Is it acceptable to tune tympani with a pitch pipe, or should you be a purist and work from a single tuning fork? More questions emerged from those sock-hops. Should I use regular sticks or those new, metal-tipped models? Should the bass drum beater strike the drum slightly above center or slightly below? Should the snare be tuned up or down, crisp or mushy?

The more involved I became in drumming, the more I felt that something was wrong. I began to see that what I really wanted wasn't popularity, but respect. Remember that joke about singers, musicians, and drummers? Drummers have always had a reputation as the dim bulbs of the music world. Imagine being in that row of guys – there weren't many girl drummers in those days – standing self-consciously in the back of the orchestra, poised to pick up something every so often and hit it. There you are, counting rests for fifteen minutes and trying not to move your lips as you wait to execute a single "ping" on the triangle, which the conductor cues with the theatrical exaggeration of a man signaling a dog to sit up. By the time you finally hit that triangle, you'll *feel* like a dog sitting up.

Playing in the rock band brought more problems. Rock drummers in the Sixties were expected to be either feral kickers or dead-eyed zombies – icons, in either case, of blood-beat intuition. Charlie Watts had the proper look, but it's hard to achieve that look if you're pudgy and pasty-faced, with Steve Allen glasses that keep slipping down your nose. I never figured out what to do with my face when I played rock. There I sat, a whirl of sticks and pedals with a useless, balloon-like face at the center of it all. I had to check a natural impulse to glance around with a wide-eyed lucidity that just didn't go with the Stones' "Satisfaction." Forcing myself to stare at an arbitrary spot in the middle distance, I chewed gum in an attempt to keep my face safely occupied.

Then there were the drum solos. Convinced that drums were meant to be accompanying instruments, I always hoped to get through the night without having to assume sole responsibility for a gymful of sweaty teenagers jumping up and down. Sooner or later, though, some idiot would cup his hands and yell "Wipeout!" and immediately the lead guitarist would launch into that mindless Surfaris hit, with its drone of monotonous sixteenth notes on the tom-toms. The crowd wanted the solo to sound just like the record, of course, and whenever I tried to make things interesting by syncopating the accents or slipping out of the old four/four throb, the dancers would buck and start like confused cattle and shoot wounded looks in my direction.

It seemed to me that only an exhibitionist could truly enjoy playing rock 'n' roll. But I wasn't drumming for glory: I didn't even like being *looked* at when I played. A junior scientist of percussion, I was a firm believer in taste and technique. My heroes were Brubeck's Joe Morello, light of touch and able to shift time signatures in a flash; that nameless, rock-steady drummer and ultimate sideman who backed James Brown; Ed Thigpen, whose subtle brushwork backed Oscar Peterson; even the oft-derided Ringo, whose simple beats and understated fills I defended as appropriately minimalist. I thought Buddy Rich shamelessly overplayed, with every arrangement a drum solo thinly disguised as a song. Dino Danelli of the Young Rascals had excellent technique, but stooped for the cheap thrill by twirling his sticks with nearly every beat. The worst offender was Ginger Baker, who was just starting to hit it big – and loud – with Cream. Surely Ginger Baker was the quintessential rock drummer, a Fortissimo Monster who abhorred even a split-second's vacuum because he failed to grasp the power of silence. But rock is a repudiation of silence, for no one more than a drummer helplessly wedged between screaming amplifiers. It was hard for me even to *think* with the fuzzy howl of an electric guitar boring into my head, my spine vibrating with the deep buzz of the electric bass.

Of course, a rock drummer shouldn't be *trying* to think, and that was my whole problem. The real cause of my discontent soon became clear: I was an embryonic jazz guy trapped in a rock 'n' roll world. The beat that came naturally to my head when I walked was not the staccato eighth-notes of rock, but an easy shuffle, the triplets and the dotted-eighths and sixteenths of the standard "ride" rhythm of jazz. Rock's endless two and four on the snare just couldn't compare with the tasty, erratic tappings of a jazz drummer's left hand.

Fortunately for me, Findlay High had the Swinging Trojans, a seventeen-piece dance band led by assistant band director Dale Rivers. Although the band, like the school's sports teams, was named after history's first losers, the Swinging Trojans at least played my kind of music. What's more, Dale Rivers tried to create my kind of atmosphere, a jazzy space where even big, goofy kids could feel like hepcats.

A trombone player in his early thirties, with black, slicked-back hair, Mr. Rivers called every playing job a "gig," even P.T.A. open-houses and the Sadie Hawkins Dance. When a set went badly, he called us "you people" like any other teacher, and spent the break outside, chain-smoking and gazing in exasperated silence at the stars. When a set went well we became "you cats." Then we could call him "Dale" and join him during the break for some jazz-guy talk about whether the piano was miked properly or which girl in the crowd was the sexiest. When we were "cats," Dale even let us bum cigarettes as he glanced nervously around to make sure no adults saw him passing them out.

One night the Swinging Trojans played the prom at Mount Blanchard, Dale's old high school. While we set up he chatted with his former teachers, his face bright red as he fumbled with the cardboard music stands. You *can* go home again, it seems, but the stakes of doing so surely get raised when the success of your homecoming hinges on the performance of seventeen rabbity kids. But we had done some extra rehearsing and were "cats" all night, outplaying ourselves as we worked through "Hawaiian War Chant," "Sing Sing Sing," "Stars Fell on Alabama," "My Funny Valentine," "String of Pearls," and everything else in our book with scarcely a blat or a miscue.

The earnings of the Swinging Trojans were supposed to go toward new uniforms for the marching band. That night, though, Dale split up the money and gave each of us a share – twenty dollars, I think. He said he was breaking the rules just this once because he wanted to teach us an important lesson: a true cat always gets paid. I was making better money than that from rock jobs, but this was different. This was *jazz*. After we got back to Findlay, a bunch of us stopped at the White Castle for bags of fifteen-cent hamburgers, sweet reward for budding jazzmen. I had trouble getting to sleep that night because "Take the A Train" kept running through my head. We had really wailed on that one.

Just when I arrived on the threshold of the jazz world, it was starting to shrink. Bill Sims soon moved to Toledo, where there were more playing jobs, and turned his students – a dozen kids whose ages ranged from six to fourteen – over to me. Between playing rock two or three nights a week and teaching on Saturday afternoons, I was saving decent money toward college. But the would-be jazz drummer plays "Louie Louie" with a heavy heart.

One day Phil McKenna, the store manager at Carter's got a call from Johnny James and the Crowns. They were looking for a drummer. I was so excited I could hardly call them back. The Crowns were the real thing: professional, adult musicians. I think they even had a listing under "Entertainment" in Findlay's Yellow Pages. When I finally called, Johnny James said that their regular drummer had suddenly left town. They had two gigs that weekend and needed a replacement fast. Did I have reliable wheels? Would I be available weeknights, too? Did I have the "chops" – that is, could I play something besides rock 'n' roll?

My audition took place at Johnny James's apartment, upstairs from James's TV Sales and Repair on West Main Cross. The bass player couldn't make it, but the pianist, Eddie Plotz, was there, and of course so was Johnny James, who came upstairs after closing the shop and immediately asked me never to call him Johnny, which was "just for publicity purposes." Mrs. James brought John and Eddie beers and gave me a Coke. I couldn't help staring at her: she was the first adult woman I had ever seen wearing bluejeans, and she was beautiful in that spooky way of beatnik folksingers. After twenty minutes of playing a few bars from different kinds of songs, John announced that I would do. He wouldn't ordinarily use a sixteen-year-old drummer, but he was in a jam. Then we rehearsed in earnest, with John and Eddie running me through their trickier numbers, including their signature tune, "What a Difference a Day Makes," which they took into a weird, a-rhythmic breakdown at the end. They closed their eyes and cocked their heads as we played, as if they were trying to concentrate on how I *sounded* rather than on how goofy I looked. I was grateful for that.

Afterwards John came out of a back room and handed me a silver sparkle tuxedo jacket and a number to call to join the musician's union. He'd been blackballed a few years back for using a nonunion kid drummer, and wasn't taking any chances. He also told me that I wasn't, under any circumstances, to drink on a job. The kid drummer had a rum-and-Coke perched on his floor tom-tom the night the union busted the Crowns. John had almost gone to jail; he escaped only by having the kid swear that it was Eddie's drink and not his. The next morning I called the American Federation of Musicians, Fostoria Local 121, and asked about auditioning for membership. A woman's tired-sounding voice told me that no audition was required. If I sent a check for twenty-five dollars, my union card and a list of clubs to boycott would arrive by return mail.

John and Eddie were representatives of a dying breed: the small-town hipster. So was Bill Sims, with his Dizzy Gillespie goatee and his wide-eyed "Oh, Man!" So was Phil at the music store, who called everything a "gas" except when he talked to parents shopping for band instruments. The era of Jack Kerouac and John Coltrane and Jackson Pollock had pretty much ended in cultural centers like New York and San Francisco, but an ideal of hipness hung on at the margins, in little towns like mine where small battles against the squares were still being fought. It was a losing effort, and a sense of being in the wrong place at the wrong time made it hard for some small-town hipsters to stay sober. Ron Dresser, the tattooed guitar teacher at the store, said he had played with "Johnny and the Hurricanes" until they fired him for smoking reefer. Ron was a jazz guy at heart, and if you remember "Johnny and the Hurricanes" – they put old chestnuts like "Red River Valley" and "Reveille" to a saxophone-and-guitar surfer beat – you might begrudge him the occasional toke. The hipster's usual drug of choice, however, was booze. Bill worried that he drank too much on jobs and kept talking about cutting back. Ron was sometimes mildly drunk even on Saturday afternoons at the store. I'd soon learn that Eddie Plotz drank a lot, too. That puzzled me: why would anyone who got paid to play music, especially jazz, ever need to get drunk?

John James, by contrast, was a jazzman in control. By day he ran the TV store, but by night he was Johnny James, a cat of the trumpet and saxophone who also sang, very occasionally, in a nondescript, lounge-guy voice. Somewhere in his late thirties, he was rail-thin and pock-marked, with blond hair combed up and flipped in an Edd "Kookie" Byrnes wave. Cool in the way that rocket scientists had been cool a decade earlier, he wore thick black-rimmed glasses with a slight maroon tint. He could wisecrack in an absolute deadpan, perfect for hissing under-the-breath insults at audience members. Whenever we were playing something slow and corny, like "Laura" or the "Tennessee Waltz," he'd turn away from the crowd and stick a finger down his throat in a mock gag. He had a collection of obscene titles that he used to call up songs he hated: "Nude River," "Nude Indigo," "I'm in the Nude for Love." I thought he was the ultimate jazz guy, surviving in these soybean hinterlands on raw talent and thick hipster irony.

Though John was a good player, I was surprised by how little he sometimes played in the course of a job. On a given night he either "had it" or he didn't. On off-nights he'd play just enough to get a song started – the first sixteen or thirty-two bars – and then drop out altogether, slackly "conducting" us with those straight jabs that Louis Prima used to make. On such nights he got moody, nervously blowing into his mouthpiece or licking his reed, endlessly moistening his lips and putting the horn to his face only to lower it again as a signal for us to cover until the set-up for each song, which he had to play the melody fairly straight, so he could take off. Whenever he finished a solid solo, he smiled thinly and cracked: "Close enough for jazz" or "Where's that advance man from Decca?"

Eddie was a hipster, too. Around John's age, he taught piano and worked in his family's hardware store. Sometimes he drank too much on our dates. For the first few sets he was fine, but then his chording would start to get sloppy and he'd play too loud. He'd get a particular riff in his head and start doing it to death, working it into every song and giggling until John had to tell him to knock it off. The only unmarried Crown (besides me, of course), Eddie occasionally tried to pick up women in the audience, always without success. John told me that Eddie once nearly cost the band a night's pay by walking up to a tall brunette and saying, "How would you like to go out with a really good piano player?" I believed it. Eddie was given to outrageous behavior – especially cursing – mostly when John told us that we had to stick to slow tunes because everybody was dancing.

Like a crisply-tuned snare drum, an ill-timed curse word will cut through all manner of noise, and nobody wants to get kicked out of the Knights of Columbus Hall because the piano player has begun swearing like a madman. It usually took a fatherly frown from the bassist to lower Eddie's voice. Herman Klein was the moral center of the Crowns. In his mid-fifties, Herm worked at the Cooper Tire plant and was the father of a shy girl in my French class. He had only three fingers on his plucking hand, the result of an industrial accident years before, but the bony stubs got a rich, full sound even in the upper registers. John gave Herm lots of solos, and he could get fancy when he had to. Unlike flashy bass players, though, he never played a run when he should have been simply "walking." His strong, steady beat freed my right foot from thumping out the old four/four on the bass drum so I could play it like a real instrument, saving it for accents and varying its dynamics. A drummer may make or break a band, but it's the bass player who makes or breaks a drummer.

We played a lot, and at lots of places: the K of C, the Armory, the Elks' Club, the VFW Hall, the Fort Findlay Lounge, Petti's Alpine Village, the Dark Horse Tavern, the Findlay Country Club, and the Eye-75 Lounge at the Holiday Inn out near the by-pass, where we had a standing gig one night a week. Sometimes we ventured out of town, to jobs in North Baltimore, Tiffin, Fremont, and Fostoria. Once we had a New Year's Eve gig beside an indoor pool at a yacht club up on Lake Erie, a five-hour job at double scale because of the holiday. That night, under the appreciative gaze of the corporate leadership of Sandusky, Ohio, I played the best drum solo of my life. Playing with the Crowns had changed my attitude toward solos. I now played them willingly, even eagerly. In a jazz solo you can explore any rhythm and texture that comes into your head, and you can even go soft, pulling the audience in with barely audible clicks and taps and hisses. I played a ten-minute solo that night, and for part of it the Crowns wandered off to the bathroom like the rock bands did. When they returned and I cued them to fall in, the crowd applauded wildly. After John flashed me a thumbs-up and said something to Eddie, they kicked into "Drummer Man," the old Krupa standard.

With tips and double-scale, I made over a hundred dollars that night. On the trip home I kept dozing off in Herm's station wagon, replaying tunes in my head and thinking that a guy might be perfectly happy doing this forever, living his life as Drummer Man. On good nights with the Crowns, the drumming felt almost entirely mental: I needed only to imagine rhythms and my hands and feet would simply *do* them. I got so I could guess where John would take a solo and echo the rhythms that Eddie would comp chords with. I could anticipate Herm, too, calculating the perfect angle on which to ride the cymbal so that his bassline and my sizzle sounded like bottom and top of a single instrument.

There's no way to describe what this felt like without sounding corny or religious, maybe both. When you're playing drums in a band that's clicking, you realize that music really *can* take you places where you wouldn't otherwise go. You can even forget, for the moment, that your skin isn't clearing up, that you still aren't smooth on dates, that your grades in English are slipping, and that you'll graduate from high school in six months, with more things to worry about than you think you'll be able to handle.

The inevitable slide from novelty to routine is one of life's first and most frequent lessons. The longer I played with the Crowns, the more clearly I could see that they had made practical choices that all working musicians must sooner or later make. They had around fifty songs in their repertoire, plenty for even the longest jobs, and instead of working up anything new, they played the classic jazzman's game of ringing changes on the old tunes. After a few months even those changes sounded stale. I began to notice that John's wildest-sounding improvisations actually combined patterns that I'd heard before – in some cases, many times before.

The Crowns were tired, partly from their day jobs but mostly from fighting a losing battle to retain a sense of hipness in a place that kept beating it down. They had caught the jazz bug, but it had doomed them to semi-irrelevance, to connecting with no one in particular. They found themselves playing either for oldsters who wanted to foxtrot and waltz or for youngsters who wanted to twist and shout. The Crowns coped with the older crowd by indulging in musical in-jokes, like sticking two bars of "Malagueña" in the middle of "Sentimental Journey." With the young crowd, people my age or a little older, they barely coped at all. Their closest approximation to rock 'n' roll was "Mississippi Mud," which Eddie played with a schmaltzy chop that was really sped-up ragtime. Herm fell in with a calypso rhythm while John issued spitty blats on the trumpet or flatulent growls on the sax. I'd try to merge Herm's calypso with Eddie's ragtime, but the young crowd always snickered. The Crowns were usually quiet afterwards. To be considered square, even by anti-jazz Luddites, was the worst fate that a small-town hipster could imagine. John tried to keep his dignity by calling the audience "bovines."

Then there were the drunks, for which Bill Sims's technical instruction definitely did not prepare me. You've just turned seventeen; you're playing a class reunion, and a beefy, red-faced man in a 1957 letter jacket grabs one of your extra sticks and starts pounding on your tom-tom. You ask him to stop and he tells you that he was a Marine and could kick your ass good. What do you do? Suppose a watery-eyed guy at a wedding reception leans into your ear and shouts that he was once a drummer and begs to sit in. What if you finally let him and he starts jabbing the sticks downward, as if he's actually *trying* to break a drumhead? Or what if a woman in her fifties, so drunk that she's been blowing kisses to John for the past half-hour, wobbles up to the stage and insists on hearing that idiotic "Mairzy Doats" song? What if John tells her that we don't know it and she looks right at *you* – the kid drummer – and orders you to play it? You smile and explain that you can't play a melody on a set of drums, but she narrows her eyes and says, "go to hell!"

The rest of the Crowns took this sort of thing in stride, but their kid drummer was made of softer stuff. While such incidents were rare, they made me darkly philosophical. A truth slowly came to me: a drummer might have his moments of transcendence on stage, but the odds were good that he'd wind up a small-town hipster, struggling to practice an art he loved but constantly hitting the unyielding wall of business, as John did whenever a club owner or, more sadly, a bride's father, tried to shortchange the band at the end of a gig. With a strange flatness in his voice, John would patiently review the fee and the number of hours of music that had been agreed upon. It was probably the same voice he used whenever someone complained about the repair bill on an old Motorola.

Whoever said "Be careful what you wish for because you might get it" must have played in a small jazz combo somewhere in the Midwest. My life as Drummer Man was petering out in disillusionment. By now I'd gotten my college acceptance, and I was surprised at how natural the thought seemed when it hit me: drumming would probably end up being little more than "something I did in high school." When I graduated and needed to make some real money for tuition at Kent State, I gave the Crowns three weeks' notice and took a summer job at the local Whirlpool plant. I brought a student of mine, a tall red-headed boy who had just turned sixteen, to a few of our gigs to break him in. He became John James's new kid drummer, and I felt a little sad when I gave him the silver sparkle tux. The Crowns were grateful that I hadn't left them in a jam, and at my last job with them, a wedding reception at the Armory, John pulled me aside and gave me a hipster's blessing: "Get some college and get out of this hole, man."

Three years later I was back in Findlay for another summer at Whirlpool. Four students had just been killed at Kent State, and I was scared and depressed. I had spent the Spring term at Southern Illinois University in an exchange program with Kent's anthropology department. The Carbondale campus shut down soon after the shootings, and I was home three weeks before Whirlpool was taking on summer help. My high school friends were either in the Army or still at schools that hadn't closed, and there was nothing to do.

One afternoon I stopped in at Carter's. Phil was leaning back in a swivel chair with his feet up on his desk, reading the latest issue of *Downbeat*. I asked him whether anyone from the old music crowd was still around. Most were gone – to college, to Cleveland, to Vietnam. When a well dressed man came in and started to tinkle the high keys of the grand piano at the front of the store, Phil straightened his tie. "This could make my month," he said with an exaggerated wink. As he approached the man at the piano he suddenly turned. "Hey, I almost forgot. Simsie's back in town. He's teaching up at the College."

When I got to the Arts Building at Findlay College I found Bill in one of the practice rooms, dozing in a metal folding chair that faced an old upright piano. I rapped on the window, and when he looked up I knew that something was wrong. He waved me in and tried to smile as I sat on a piano bench, but he looked terrible. His skin, formerly a rich brown, was now yellow with greenish shadows. He slurred his words and seemed to have a hard time keeping his eyes open. I asked if he was okay and he said he was just tired. He was teaching more and playing less because nobody wanted to hear jazz anymore. He asked how school was going and we made some small talk, and after a while he cleared his throat and said he had to get ready for a percussion class. As I got up, he stayed in the chair and took my hand, looking up with a sleepy smile and slowly turning his head from side to side, like he did when he played. I said we'd have to get together this summer and jam, like in the old days. He squeezed my hand and said I'd have to go because of his class.

The next week I started what would be my last gig. A woman from Columbus had called Phil at the store. Her name was Maria and she needed a drummer to back her on Saturday nights. Although I hadn't really played since high school, I was desperate to fill up my time. Phil told me to show up at the Dark Horse Tavern at seven-thirty that Saturday with my set and a dark sportcoat. The job paid thirty dollars a night, plus tips if Maria was willing to share them.

The Crowns had played the Dark Horse several times. It was one of those wood-paneled, vaguely Alpine restaurant-bars that once could be found in every small Midwestern town. Findlay College kids sometimes went there on dates, but the crowd mostly consisted of middle-aged office guys from Marathon Oil and Cooper Tires treating their wives to a special prime rib, which always came medium when you ordered it rare. The lighting was a little dimmer than was comfortable for eating. Once your eyes got used to the darkness, you could make out a faded painting behind the bar: a black horse rearing up next to a beer stein.

Maria, a large woman in a spangly cocktail dress and an immense bluish wig, was sitting at the bar when I showed up. Like John James, she immediately asked how old I was and whether I was in the union. Not yet willing to let go of my drumming identity completely, I had kept up my dues. As I handed her my card she said she didn't like working with kids and she didn't play rock 'n' roll. Could I deal with that? I'd have to use brushes most of the time. Could I deal with *that?* Remembering this drill from my initial grilling by the Crowns, I told her I loved brushes because you could play badly and nobody would notice. She took a deep drag from her cigarette – it was in a holder – and glared at me. "Uh-huh."

When I told her I had taken lessons from Bill Sims, her mouth dropped open in mock surprise. "Honey, why didn't you *say* so? Bill Sims and me go way back." When Bill was just out of high school they had played together in a small combo in Columbus. I told her how awful he looked at the College, and she vowed to drive up early some Saturday and see him. Smiling now, she removed her cigarette from the holder and stubbed it out. "Go set yourself up." As I got up from the barstool she took my elbow. "Honey, I'm a sideman's dream. You back me good, the tips go fifty-fifty. Maria never stiffed nobody." Within a half hour she was easing into that old Crowns' favorite,

"What a Difference a Day Makes," in front of my steady – and very soft – brushwork.

I backed Maria every Saturday night that summer. Nearly thirty years of playing lounges had hardened her to the wearisome task of entertaining people whose tastes were not hers. She knew how to work a room, how to stack and pace a set, how to make music that wouldn't intrude on table conversations. She had developed a sizable repertoire of snappy patter that grew increasingly risqué as the evening went on and the diners were gradually replaced by the drinkers. But Maria had drawn one uncrossable line: whenever a Findlay College student requested a rock song, she'd lean into the mike and say, "I got a better idea, Honey – how about some *music*?" In her sole concession to the times, she had worked up a few of the softer Beatles numbers, which came out sounding like Errol Garner tunes.

Between Saturday nights at the Dark Horse and my night shift at Whirlpool, I saw almost no one all summer, no mean feat in a close little place like Findlay. That was fine with me. After the shootings, what I needed more than anything else was privacy to work things out without being watched. That Toledo psychologist might not have approved, but I wanted to be invisible. A small spotlight shining down on Maria threw everything around her in deep shadows. That's where I sat, with only the outer edge of my ride cymbal protruding into the light. I could not recall being in a safer place.

The only time anyone I knew came into the Dark Horse was one night when I recognized one of my high school gym teachers, Tony Antolini, making his unsteady way toward the bathroom. He was so drunk his eyes weren't focused. As he passed the stage he stopped and peered into the darkness behind the cymbal. "I know you, man," he said, "don't tell me." After snapping his fingers a few times, he convinced himself that I was an old fraternity brother from Bowling Green whose name he couldn't remember. There was no telling him otherwise, so I finally said that he was right and that my name was Jerry Hamilton. "That's right! Hey man, I *knew* it! He yelled back at a table of beefy guys that this was his frat brother Jerry here, playin' the freakin' drums and everything. Maria laughed and said that these hick towns always brought out the best in everyone. "Those dear hearts and gentle people, Honey."

Not long after the "Tony A" episode, I saw in the paper that Bill Sims had died of liver failure. That Saturday, when I told Maria the news, she went to the bar and bought two shots of bourbon. I was still underage, so I followed her as she carried the drinks through the kitchen and out the back door. Standing next to a dumpster in the golden light of early evening, we drank to Bill's memory. When we were back inside and about to start the first set, she switched on her mike and announced that tonight's music would be dedicated to Bill Sims. Then she turned to me and whispered, "Give me a good drummer song." I thought for a few seconds. "Caravan."

She nodded, and as we started into it the patrons – still mostly the dinner crowd – looked up from their conversations. As was proper for a song like "Caravan" and a farewell to Bill Sims, I had put down the brushes and was using sticks, which thumped on the tom-toms and filled the room with sounds that could not, by any stretch of the imagination, be called "dinner music." A few of the younger people on dates began calling for their checks. But several older, married-looking couples got up and started an easy jitterbug, urged on by Maria's patter but driven more deeply by an impulse that I never really understood until many years later, long after I had given up drumming for other things.

....Jeffrey Hammond

*One step in preparing for the next millennium is to remember that
while on some people's calendar – the Christian one – this may be a
turn of time loaded with symbolism, it's just another year in the
Islamic, Jewish, Buddhist, etc., calendars – And to the DNA in our
cells or the red-shift of the stars, it's just a millisecond ticking in the
long clock of time.*

....*Minnie Bruce Pratt*

*The distance between our work and our lives is often an invisible
border – one we cannot see or simply refuse to see. Our creativity is
what encourages us to seek shelter and understanding in new worlds.
Too often we cannot return to the old land, language, or even memory.
To be a poet is to love, to pursue desire, to soar above the landscape
and territory of flags and anthems. There is a hunger in the heart of
almost every man and woman. How many hands must we push away
from our mouths as we enter the 21ˢᵗ century?*

....*E. Ethelbert Miller*

The Old Trains

the old politicians wore vests with golden watch chains
   and they smoked cigars in the Pullmans crossing the plains
the old politicians were fat they swore and spat
   but at the stations they smiled and forswore swearing
and went to waving at multitudes and praying

since the multitudes were simple citizens mostly
   housewives lovers sheriffs and cardsharks mostly
who came to the stations to hear a few words from rear platforms
   about their futures
for the multitudes always clapped and cheered for their futures

for their futures were always golden like golden watch chains
   or like sunsets over the peaks toward which the old trains
steamed always westward westward
   for futures were always westward and would have been golden
but for the villains

but always between the stations were secretive boulders
   behind which lurked villains
who yearned for the golden watch chains and gold in the mail cars
   they were smart too those villains with golden futures
between stations

if only the futures had stayed safe in the stations
   with the old politicians waving and praying from platforms
and if only the villains picking up gold in the Pullmans
   hadn't winked at the old politicians swearing and spitting,
then the heroes....

               the heroes? what about heroes?

yes somewhere along the very long line between stations
   the heroes had jumped from the Pullmans and rustled up horses
and changed their heroic duds behind secretive boulders
   yes somewhere along the line the heroes had winked
at the old politicians
                    so let us not speak of heroes

                                        ....Reed Whittemore

Requiem

after Chukovskaya

In my time I have had to flee twice.
As I fled I knew what I was running from and why.
I was standing at the window of a train watching the platform
sail past me, thinking of the morning's friendly telephone call,
our own clumsily crafted lives.
Who could have guessed the content of my days, whispers,
guesses, real life omitted, just faint glimmers here & there, a hint
of it, some sign, some future which was never to be –
Residue of sleepless nights, little squares of the parquet floor,
my daughter, I felt I had to stay alive for her –
What documents was I keeping and where....
Sometimes, in mid-conversation, silence, followed
by something very mundane – "Would you like some tea?" "You're
very tanned," "Autumn came early this year, – "
The bookcase, the writing desk, the clock –
chiseling out of this some beautiful and mournful ritual.

....Jane Satterfield

Mommy's Bracelet

Michael Millner,
I dedicate this poem
to you.
Michael Millner,
we have not
forgotten you.

Mommy's bracelet;
stainless steel wrapped
around her left wrist,
just below her watch.
There is a space where
the two ends meet, curved
metal just barely touching.

I am six: I trace
the letters engraved
on the metal, pretend
it is Braille, too young
to read with eyes open.
"What does it say Mommy?
Is it from Daddy?
Is it about me?"

Mommy pulls her hand
away and looks at her
wrist, as if checking
the time.
"It says S/FC Michael Millner.
11/29/67.
It's not from Daddy.
It's not about you."

"But who is Michael...?"

She does not answer, looking
at something far away, or not
looking at all.
She is quiet.

I grow quiet.

I am thirteen: in school,
we are learning about
the Vietnam War. 1967...
I ask again about her bracelet.

"It's a POW/MIA bracelet.
Thousands were given out
during and after the war –
police action. We're not
to take them off until
something is found –
dogtags, papers...remains –
and they are no longer
lost." She holds the
bracelet, wrapping the fingers
of her right hand around
it, around her wrist.

"Is there a bracelet for everyone
who was lost? How do you know
if they were found? What
if they don't want to be
found? Will I inherit
the bracelet?"

She sets her book down
in front of her. "Sometimes,

if they find...someone,
it's in the newspaper. I check.
I'm sure he would want to be
found; he has a wife and
two children. I don't
know if you will inherit
it – let's hope they find him."
She looks at her wrist again,
briefly, then picks up the book.

I am twenty-two and I
am writing a poem about
my mother's bracelet.
I call her, asking for
the date on it; the name
I still remember.
She reads it to me
over the phone, then asks
"Do you want to know
the rest?"

Michael Millner had just
signed up for another
tour when he was reported
missing.
Michael Millner's two children,
four and six when he was lost,
both needed counseling,
both needed to hear that Daddy may
never come home, but not
because he didn't love
them, or because they had done
something wrong.
Michael Millner's wife
years after his disappearance

was engaged; she spent
seven years looking at herself
each night in the mirror,
not knowing if she was
a widow
or an adulteress; she
broke the engagement.

When the Wall in Washington
was dedicated, Michael Millner's
son marched in the honor guard,
proudly wearing the uniform
his father once wore, may still wear,
may be buried in.

"Do they still find people Mom?
Do you ever take the bracelet off?"

"Sometimes in the paper
it will say they found
a mass grave in a barn
somewhere, or a soldier
who'd gone native, married
a local girl, disappeared.

"No, I don't take it off."

Michael Millner, my mother
wears your name
just over her steady pulse.
Each time she looks at her watch
to check the time
she sees decades
thirty-two years of
stainless steel
trying to seal the gaps in

her generation in
her faith in
the world.

Michael Millner
we have not
forgotten you.
Michael Millner
I dedicate this poem
to you.

.....*Lauri Watkins*

The Wave

Memorial Stadium, Baltimore, 1991

Vendors with racks of soft drinks, palettes
of cotton candy, ice cream in bright insulated
bags, pretzels in metal cabinets, and the peanut
man with his yellow peanut earring. Money folded

between fingers, spokes of green waving
in the glad pandemonium greeting the Budman
with his quick-pouring mechanism strapped
to his wrist like a prosthesis, or the hot-dog guy

genuflecting in the steep aisles, anointing
the roll and weenie with mustard before passing
it down to the skinny kid sitting between fat parents.
In the air above us the flittering birds attracted

and repelled by planetary field lights, swoop
in ecstatic arcs, trapped under a dark invisible dome.
The park organ, the Jumbo-tron, the mascot
pacing atop the visitors' dugout, taunting them

with over-sized antics, while the groundskeepers
spray the infield with a fire hose, leavening
the calm, raked earth... Later, in the fifth
or sixth, two soldiers sitting next to me, who

have paced each other with a beer-an-inning and kept
their buzz buffed with a flask, take off their shirts,
though the night's cool, and move to the front row,
where they turn, face the crowd, and sweep up

their arms, commanding us to rise from our seats.
At first only a few respond, but like molecules quickening
or cells dividing or a herd stampeding, we coalesce –
orison provoking unison – section by section, as if

township by township, our standing up and sitting down,
becomes the Simon Says and Mother-May-I? of a nation,
as it runs through our rippling, shimmering, upraised hands
that form the crest of a wave built on the urges

and urgings of the soldiers whose skin is slick
with sweat or some other laborious issue and whose goal
now, for all of us, for themselves, for the players on the field,
is simply to stay in the wave, to keep it going for as long as they can.

....*Michael Collier*

What Grandma Said

Once Grandma told me she was afraid of dying,
a great secret since church was her avocation.
At the time she was standing
in the scarred doorway, lintels
much-painted to cover the stabs
of sabre and knives
from the Civil War,
between her kitchen
with its black iron stove,
and the dining room
where she often sat by the radio
in a rocking chair, tatting, the tiny shuttle
flying magically as she made lace.

By then, the Civil War was far back in time,
and the fact soldiers had been billeted
in this oldest part of the house,
that it had been used as a hospital,
this familiar space part of a battleground,
astonished me,
the smell of blood and fear
long replaced with the aroma of roasts
and pies from the range.

When I was older, I imagined Walt Whitman,
a nurse in the War, in this room,
his beautiful piercing eyes,
the beard hiding his poems,
that old lilac at Grandma's back door,
the one of which he wrote – who knows,
the fantasy was sweet.

But that Grandma was afraid of dying,
of Heaven, the aftermath of her life,
after all those Sundays at church on her knees
frightened me, as it touched me,
for by then she had lost so many,
too many to count,
But Grandma was human.
Thank God she could not foresee
the future that day, as she rallied her faith,
proclaiming her desire to die with her boots on,
(her phrase, military, fitting,
in that old battle-room), couldn't know
that she was doomed to die
two deaths instead of one,
fated to lie in the twilight of coma
for seven years before the blessed respite
of death finally came.

.....Irene Rouse

I try to be a poet in the world, delighting in language. But, there is this cultural baggage, the pajamas of skin that you want to zip up and take off. That's not about black skin. That's about waking up with the man. That is something else. I delight in my color and my culture. What I do walk away from is the historical baggage of how the white man sees me.

....Fred D'Aguiar

Embracing the millennium surely means moving into it with love. It means moving into it with confidence and hope, with some kind of vision of what we want to become as a people on this bright blue planet.

....Sara Ebenreck

The week had kept turning corners that left Russell facing the past. Yesterday, interrogating a twenty year old white male named Jason Waxman who was suspected of dealing crack cocaine at the high school, he had inadvertently joked in Vietnamese with Trung, a California-born deputy. Trung had looked at him blankly: he affected not to speak a word. But the suspect had gone pale at the sound of the language. "You're a vet," he had said.

Russell found himself offended at the boy's fear.

"What are you, a cocker spaniel? You need to be altered?"

"You know what I mean."

He had put Waxman's thumb between his own thumb and forefinger, the boy's flesh white as bone against his skin. At the gentle squeeze he gave, Waxman began to talk. He was scared to death. Russell had learned long before that being offended by a stereotype didn't mean you shouldn't use it.

Now he was driving to Point Lookout to help in the search for a sixteen year old half-black, half-Vietnamese girl named Kiet who had run away from a residential program for troubled adolescent girls.

He was taking his time. He doubted that Kiet would come in this direction; usually when girls went AWOL from the counseling center they headed north, to DC or Baltimore. But a figure, female, had been spotted wading out at the Point, and the cold water was being dragged and searched by divers.

The girls, often inner-city kids, hated being sent to the boonies, and where he was now was the least populated area of the county: a crust of houses, white clapboard churches and country stores along the highway, beyond them fields and forest and marsh. The further south you went, the narrower the peninsula became until finally the Potomac and the Bay pinched out the land between them; that tip of the county was Point Lookout. The state had started from here, back in 1634, and so, in a sense, had he: the progenitor of his own family – a slave named Lucius from Dahomey via Barbados, had come with the British ship Ark to this place, bought by a carpenter named Hallam: a fact Russell's boss Alex Hallam, white, that man's descendent, regarded with an amusement that Russell didn't know how to take.

Alex believed, Russell knew, that he was spiked and fastened by his obsession with family history. But he didn't believe he had the choice Alex implied. He had been born, like many in his family, with twelve fingers; the extra two had been amputated when he was a baby. But he still felt the invisible ache of them on his hands, organs of an extra sense that dipped and stirred into time. Time touched him back. It wasn't a matter of searching it out. It was simply there, the weight of an internal presence. It was something the Vietnamese would probably understand: their ancestry and history were felt as points of reference, of lookout, in a person's soul. Though Kiet, the child he was looking for, black GI father she never knew, Vietnamese mother, only had a history of running away.

He was nearly at the beginning of the state park now. On impulse, he stopped at the memorial to the Confederate dead, an obelisk with the names of the dead inscribed on copper plates fastened around its base. Over thirty-five thousand prisoners had been kept at the Point Lookout camp, some of them rebel sympathizers from the county. Thousands of men had died here, of disease, exposure, maltreatment. The prisoners had been packed into flimsy tents and slept on the ground: the country was marshy and unhealthy and exposed to ill winds off the Chesapeake Bay and the river. Many must have died, he supposed, of broken hearts: to the west, on the Potomac side, they would have stood and stared at the shoreline of Virginia, as distant and as tantalizing as the shores of heaven. He imagined it added to their sense of hell that often their guards were ex-slaves who had joined the Union army: the prisoners' and in fact the Union officers' diaries that he had read expressed horror that black troops had been set over Confederate prisoners. His family had a story about an ancestor who had been a guard and who had either abused or murdered a white Hallam, his former master. He had never been able to confirm the story in any of the histories. Perhaps it was only wishful thinking.

In Vietnam, when he had briefly been a guard at a POW compound himself, he had tried to relate the experience to Point Lookout. But the Vietnamese prisoners, mostly starved amputees, were poor substitutes for white Southerners, and the job had only caused him to lose the romantic image he had of the VC as supermen. Their filth, lethargy and indifference had infuriated him. When he knew he'd murder someone if he had to keep looking at their faces, he'd gotten a transfer back to a line unit.

The mist draped around the monument and paled the bright green of the pines behind the iron-picket fence that enclosed the area. A moldy smell clogged his nostrils and the cone of air around him turned suddenly icy, a spot he could move out of, he found, by taking a step to the right or left. He wondered if it were a trick of air currents or if his presence had stirred something.

He walked to the needle, put his hand down flat, over some names. The coldness of the metal moved into his palm. He had been once, only once, to the Wall in Washington. Standing at its apex, he had felt he was winging out from his own center, the names carved inside him. He couldn't stay. But the names on this monument, even the familiar county names his fingers traced now, meant nothing to him. More than nothing: he was glad they were dead.

He looked for Hallam, as he had before, but again he couldn't find his own name on the monument.

He left the memorial and drove south, passing the signs for the camping ground and Civil War museum, set back in the tall loblolly pines to the right of the narrow road. On the other side were several weather-beaten frame houses, their yards weedy, the knobbed silver globe of a sea-mine on a pedestal in one front yard. Then the country opened suddenly, and it was as if he were driving into water, passing from one element to the other, the road on top of a narrow stone berm, the Bay vast and gray and seething with white caps on his left, Lake Conoy, a large pond that flowed into the Potomac on his right. He could see the river glinting through a thin tall picket of loblollies on the eastern edge of the pond. At the end of the causeway, on the Bay side, was a brief wedge of grass between the road and the water. A spoked iron wheel stood half-buried near a picnic table. He stopped the car again, stalling, not sure why.

He got out. A boy was standing on the edge of the rocks near the grass, throwing a baited line out into the water. It was the wrong time of year for crabs, but the boy's concentrated stillness tugged a memory out of Russell; when he was a kid, crabbing, he would stand like that, a dip net in one hand, the other delicately holding the end of a trot line, pulling his thoughts from the gray flowing of the water. He touched the iron of the wheel, wondering if it were an object from the camp. It held a different coldness than the monument's: the coldness of the water in which it had lain. The land had steadily eroded since the prison had been here; during the war the shoreline here extended out perhaps half a mile into the Bay. On the horizon, he saw a ship, a freighter headed towards Baltimore, drawing a line between sky and sea. He looked at the near water. It was cold and dark and smoothly heavy, heaving itself up, pushing against the shore.

Under the surface here would be more ruins, broken plates, chains, mini-balls, the barnacle-encrusted bones of unburied white prisoners clicking against the bones of the Middle Passage that had marched here along the ocean's bottom compelled to complete their journey, to push blindly against the mass of the continent. He tried to imagine the girl, Kiet's face, emerging suddenly, half-black, half-Vietnamese, his own past made into a construct, rising, water streaming from eye sockets and astonished mouth. A shadow passed under his gaze; he started, then grinned at himself as he recognized the surprisingly graceful flap and glide, a glimpsed motion that gave his imagination just enough to fill in the form of the ray. He let himself glide under the surface with it, the cold water smooth over him, his bottom eyes probing the dark rocks and silt, a sediment thick with secrets and crimes, his slit ears straining to hear voices, the stories, the one unknown story still held locked like another bone in the bottom mud. A distinct word rose and opened in his mind, as perfectly as a bubble.

Hallam.

I am considered an educated man for one of my race, although Dr. Miles Oberle, my former mentor at the New England Conservatory for Freed Africans would undoubtedly chide me for the above phrase. You are simply an educated man, he would say. I have found, however, that while simplicity is much to be desired, it is rarely achieved and the qualification I make perhaps stems from the way I have come to regard myself. For if one thinks of education as enlightenment, of light, the pure *lux* (from the Greek leukos, white) which overcomes darkness then I cannot help but think of myself as that which must be overcome.

Lux et logos. Those gilted words, engraved above the door of Dr. Oberle's study, his sanctum sanctorum, will always conjure the Conservatory to me. *Lux* illuminated *logos. Lux* was the cool New England light that flowed like a blessing through the bay windows and touched a muted gleam from the polished oak furniture and floors, that awakened a warm smell, like that emanating from milk-fed, content animals nuzzling in a clean barn, from the leather-bound books lining the shelves. *Lux* glittered from the golden titles branded onto their spines. At certain times of the day, rainbow prisms of light would sparkle from the fine crystal in the red China closet, while at others, globules of lemony light would move like luminous spirits over the portraits of the Fathers, Washington and Jefferson, framed on the walls, decoalesce and drip onto the blindly staring marble busts of the great thinkers: Socrates, Plato, Aristotle, Descartes. That room was to me the physical formulation of logos itself. Even the mahogany fireplace mantelpiece, which was decorated with a bas relief of elephants and gilded Negro heads, their widened eyes gleeful with stupidity, their thick-lipped mouths, drooped open like idiot children's, seemed contained, made ridiculous and safe by the room, which of course was Dr. Oberle's intent in having it there. The design, he told me, was copied from the decoration over the door of the Liverpool Customs House and was emblematic of the slave trade: it was commonly said by the English themselves in those days that Liverpool's streets were marked out by chains, the bricks of its houses cemented with African blood. This too is conquered, Oberle wanted the decoration to say, conquered by the fact he dared put it there, conquered by what surrounded it: those paintings, those sculpted heads, the reasoned words standing in tight-shouldered solidarity on the book shelves. I found it impolitic to mention the obvious paradox that the right hand, so to speak, could sculpt one set of heads while the left carved those repulsive visages.

He was after all, my mentor. I had come to the Conservatory soon after I ran away from south Maryland in March of 1858, in my seventeenth year. In May of that same year, I had been asked to address an Abolitionist meeting of Boston Common, a gathering attended by Dr. Oberle. My quick tongue was married to my thick ignorance, a combination which drew him to me; I suppose I seemed backwards enough to benefit from his aid, yet gifted with enough natural eloquence to promise his success. At his request, we were introduced after the rally; he asked me if I could read and write (I could. Even though it was illegal, I had been taught the art at my old master's bidding, for he liked to have me read to him in the evenings). Soon after that interview, Oberle invited me to join the dozen or so other students, all runaway slaves, he had chosen to bring to the light.

For the most part, I remember my time at the Conservatory with fondness; it was a flowing and tranquil passage. There are only two incidents that jar my memory. The first occurred, of all places, in Bible class. I cannot be certain why that occasion has stayed in my mind except that it marked an unusual agitation in me about a subject which had never been one I had taken with any seriousness before, my mind tending towards the rational and scientific. That day Dr. Oberle was visiting the class, which was taught by the Reverend Silas Gough; the subject was Abraham begetting a child in his old age. According to Dr. Gough, faith in the possibility of the miraculous was one message we could extract from this incident.

But what of Ishmael, I found myself asking, my voice to my surprise, to the astonishment of the others in the room (Dr. Gough stroking his beard, looking at Dr. Oberle, who stroked his own in a mirroring response), suddenly cracking with emotion. I had learned by then – I was near graduation – to affect a dispassionate coolness sharpened with just an edge of sarcasm as my persona, and the rage that seized me was, to say the least, unexpected. How could a father abandon his own child, and that child's mother, to what he surely must have thought would have been certain death in the desert, simply because Ishmael was the child of a slave? I demanded. Was he not still Abraham's son. Only, to my further consternation, I realized I had not phrased my question in these words; in my agitation I slipped back into myself. "He not be Abraham chile?" I asked. Stopping myself, looking at the startled faces around me, looking startled myself at the words that had slipped past my lips like traitors, I suddenly realized that I had risen to my feet and was shouting.

I sat down, shamefaced, my hands trembling. The extended point of the passage, Mr. Hallam, Dr. Gough said quietly, is that this miracle made Abraham the progenitor of the Hebrews, who thus could fulfill their mission of becoming the human progenitors of the Christ, the light of the world. If Abraham's blessing had gone to Ishmael, this symbolically would signify the victory of the baser forces of his nature that had resulted in the child of the lower state. Yet to leave a child in the desert, I began, but stopped when I saw the impatience clouding his face, the disappointment in the eyes of Dr. Oberle. There is always the danger, Mr. Hallam, he said, of losing one's objectivity.

That Bible class had been my last before graduation and for a time I worried that my indiscretion might threaten my being chosen as valedictorian. But it did not.

Commencement took place in Dr. Oberle's study. There were but twelve of us in Dr. Oberle's graduating class that year, and to a man we enlisted in the 36th United States Colored Infantry, under Colonel A. G. Draper. I began my speech by announcing that enlistment with a beaming pride that produced a ripple of emotion from my audience. We needed, I said, as we went forth to battle, to call that we were going to be engaged in a conflict unlike any other fought in the history of mankind, a struggle engendered not from greed, not from the coveting of a neighbor's goods and chattels, nor even from a desire to break the chains of tyranny from oneself, like the struggles of the slave Spartacus or the valiant Hasmoneans. No, I maintained, here, for the first time in human history, was a battle motivated by the purest altruism, for what else could we name it when the men of one race were willing to give their lives, to fight their own brothers, in order to liberate those of another race?

As we took our position in the ranks, I admonished, when the applause had ceased, we needed to nourish our astonishment at this sacrifice in order to save ourselves from the monster of vindictive hatred that could destroy us, even in our moment of victory. We, the sons of Ham, had eaten the bitter herbs of slavery, yet – we needed to remember – without that original taste, we would not be here either: the light of *logos* would have been denied us if we'd remained in our baser, native state, exiled in the desert. White hands had rudely plucked us from that state, I said, my metaphors becoming somewhat confused in my excitement at the approval my speech was gaining; white hands had placed us in harsh servitude, yet white hands also – I nodded to the audience – had reached down and picked us up to the sun of truth and civilization. Thus, even as we fought our oppressors, we must never forget to guard against becoming like them through blind hatred and the facile satisfaction offered by retribution. In the words of Thomas Paine, I concluded, (I knew my audience) tyranny, like hell, is not easily conquered.

As I spoke, I kept my eye on Dr. Oberle, the faculty, the trustees of the institute. Their murmurs of approval, their pale hands stroking their beards with increasing speed, as if to gauge an inner pleasure, warmed me. In a theatrical manner even the day itself joined the ceremony: a beam of light flowed through the windows, illuminating, as if to paint into my memory, the details of that room. It fell on the shelves of books, it fell on the Persian carpet, on the richly gleaming oak furniture and then, inevitably, it fell on that accursed mantelpiece.

As the row of wooly headed, mocking faces suddenly blazed before my eyes, each became a black, metastasizing cell of doubt entering my body. These fathers nodding at me, these graybeards, had brought both of us to this room and I wondered suddenly at their intent in lining us before them, as into crooked mirrors. They had brought us into their light, these white men, but they had also fashioned these heads, we were both their children and neither of us their inheritors. Was this truly such a mystery to me, who knew it in my flesh that a hand that could caress and stroke could also rend and tear? Those gaped mouths called to me: who do you think you are, pickaninny, parrot, gibbering ape, what do you think you are doing here? I tried to force my gaze from them, but I turned my head and they melted into the faces of the faculty and trustees, faces suddenly anxious at my silence, mouths suddenly murmuring with concern instead of approval, and the metamorphosis continued so that I saw black flesh fall away and their whiteness became a row of grinning skulls that parodied the mocking African faces.

Finally, the growing mutter caused me to shake my head, shake off the vision, and I continued. But the applause when I finished my speech was more an outburst of relief than of admiration.

My graduation from the conservatory merged into a different form of education, that of the training camp, but I cheerfully endured its mindless brutality for I felt it was suffered to hone me for a nobler purpose. The earlier lessons of my slavery, which for the main part consisted of a protective retreat into expected mannerisms, came back to me at this time; they were of great value in my intercourse with my drill sergeant and white officers. At the end of our training period, we were read the news of the great scrap at Gettysburg and we became fearful the war would be over soon. I was wild with impatience, eager not to miss the tide of history.

To my disappointment, though, the 36th did not march to be tested in the crucible of battle. Instead, we were to be sent to Southern Maryland, the very place where I had endured my slavery, the cursed ground where I had buried my mother and promised myself not to return. But I was a soldier now; I had willingly sacrificed the freedom I'd taken to myself in order to extend and ennoble it. I had to, to put it simply, follow orders. The whites of the region, certainly not to my surprise, were sympathetic to the Secesh, and Federal troops that had to be sent to occupy the area both in order to catch blockade runners and also to control the spies and saboteurs this poisonous pocket of rebellion spewed northwards. In addition, a large prison depot had been built at Point Lookout just miles south of Scotland, where I had spent my years of servitude and we were to help garrison it. Although the Second regiment of New Hampshire Volunteers was already deployed at the depot, its population was growing due to the Confederacy's defeat at Gettysburg. And perhaps it was felt (although perhaps it could be the War Department was reluctant to trust us in battle) that justice would be served by assigning a regiment of colored troops as guards of their former keepers.

And so, in the beginning of May in the year 1863, behind the flags of regiment and country, I marched as official and unrelenting as a debt back to the place where I was born. There was something of the dream about it: in my uniform, armed, I moved down into a land devastated as if by the fire of my hatred. Fields had gone to weed or were growing up in pine trees; dogs and cattle were running wild. When we came to Leonardtown, the county seat, the buildings were closed, their windows boarded, and bony pigs were rooting in the main street. There were very few people who came out to see us, though I looked into every white face as if peering into a mirror, searching for the one face I knew as I knew my own to form before my eyes. But we passed only old men and women who stared at our black faces as if we had marched out of their own uneasy dreams. Only old men and women: they kept the children and the young women hidden and their able menfolk had gone to Virginia to join the rebels.

We marched south, down through the St. Inigoes district, until we passed Scotland. It was a name that, before my eyes were opened to geography, had meant only this hot, lowland place to me.

The prison camp spread itself below Scotland and onto the Point, exposed to wind and water on that sandy spit. Before us were the neat dwellings of the guard regiments, the sturdily fashioned and well maintained administrative and supply buildings and then, beyond them, a deadline ditch, a rampart and a city of rotting white canvas tents, acres of tents so ragged in appearance that they had the aspect of patches of diseased skin, scaling off the land. They covered the country of my childhood.

What I have kept all these years since is a stink in my nostrils and pictures, daguerreotypes fastened behind my mind's eye, flash burned into my brain. Pictures. A group of emaciated prisoners arriving at the wharf, my fellow guards, ex-slaves ennobled by their suffering, tearing the rags from the backs of these wretches and throwing that clothing into the Bay, so these white men stood naked in the wind, as on an auction block or an African beach. The malodorous mud alleys between the tents, puddled with urine and piled with lumps of excrement. A Negro guard shooting a squatting, bare-bottomed prisoner driven into the night by the diarrhea all of them had. A stocky, sturdy New Hampshire man shooting down with cold rage a Confederate officer who taunted him that Yankees and niggers, all guards, all in the same uniform, must be equal. Shooting him for the utterly offensive insult of that remark, this New England soldier on my side of the war. Another prisoner, a gaunt, bearded mean with fiery eyes, a patriarchal figure who reminded me of lithographs I had seen of John Brown, stepping deliberately into the deadline ditch and Jim Tanner, the ex-field slave from Mississippi who had dared him to do it, just as deliberately shooting him in the head. Tanner. Tanner making prisoners driven from their tents by dysentery get on their knees and pray "fo President Lincoln and the colored folks," making them carry him on their backs as he whooped, his mud-stained, red-rimmed eyes rolling at me, fixed to mine, smiling his mockery at my look of disgust, his face one of the faces I had seen on the mantelpiece. Tanner.

He was my guide into this new country that my old country had rolled over into as if in some inexorable balancing of nature's justice. On my first day, he brought me with him into the prisoners' area. The prisoners scurried out of his way, disappearing into their tents as he walked the mud streets. Tanner was Provost Marshal Brady's favorite; he had gotten away with murder more than once, and they knew it. As we walked, he recited information about the layout of the camp, the rules involving relief of guard, the deadline, the contraband market (yes there was commerce in hell, surely no surprise to a former slave. I have heard that Major Brady, called Beast, left the Point with over a million dollars in his retirement fund). The prisoners, Tanner told me, were permitted twelve ounces of hard bread a day; if they had greenbacks they could always buy more. Or they could scavenge.

"It seems hardly enough for a man to live on, sergeant," I said.

Tanner turned to me. The weave of tiny veins that formed a scraggly red border around his eyes seemed to glow (old bloodeye the prisoners, and many guards for that matter, called him, when he was not within hearing). A slow smile spread on his face, "Why you talk so white, nigger?" he asked.

"I have had schooling," I said stiffly.

He laughed. When he spoke, he seemed to exaggerate the discrepancies of his language. "Well, le'me tell you somephin, School. Lose some sixty a day, fum de scurvy. We got bowt twenty-thousand take care ob. Scurvy too damn slow." He peered at me curiously. "I just gib dem dey amount. Set dey amount. You know about de amount, boy? Where you slave?"

"Here."

He laughed even louder. But the red glow stayed in his eye, smoldering like a choice he kept at hand under the choice he seemed to have made of being amused at me.

"Firs' day, field handin, I mus be six, seben year ol', dey gib me a sack," Tanner said. "Got a strap roun my neck, my mowth open, mowth a de sack open at my heart, bottom a de sack drag de ground. Also got dis basket, for when de sack full. Dey say pick, I pick. I pick, dey whip all de time fus day, cause what I doing, I settin my amount. Dat day my amount one hunnert pound. Dey nevah see no six, seben year old do one hunnert pound. Dat day on, at end a picking ebery day, you go down the Gin House, weigh up. Undah you amount, dey whip you up. Obah you amount, dey figger you fake befo, whip you up too, next day you pick dat much. Understand, School? You wanna see mah back, times I ovah or undah mah amount?"

"I have an amount that I havev carried also, sergeant," I said (what a pompous ass I was in those days). "But I believe we must be better than they are."

The red net glowed. "Bettah. You right dere, School."

He spun around. His quickness caught a man who had been standing in the shade of a tent, eavesdropping on our conversation. I had not thought that Tanner had seen him. The prisoner was still wearing the bedraggled uniform of a Confederate captain. He stared at us strangely. He had a long, thin face and his rotted teeth, elongated by the retraction of his gums, gave it a horse cast. He looked back and forth at our faces, then nodded and laughed to himself.

Tanner nodded also. "Come on ovah heah, Cap'n Norris," he said.

The man shrugged and pulled something from his pocket. He held it up in front of his face as he approached us, snapping it between his hands. A greenback. When his breath washed over me, I understood why he had not ducked back into his tent like the others.

"You look like a damned old whiskeyhead, sergeant," he said, swaying. "Why don't you take this, go buy me some whiskey. From your massa, the Beast. Got fetch me some beast whiskey. Some hairy beast brew."

When he was finished, he stood, a sneer forming on his lips, then disappearing, then forming, as if he were tugged between fear and insolence. As if a part of him were remembering to be afraid.

"Dis man talkin contraband, School," Tanner said. "You head him?"

"Sergeant, a little philanthropy is all I ask," Norris gave a mock bow. "Aren't you a philanthropist, sergeant? You look ripely philanthropic to me."

"You callin me what?" Tanner said, putting a hand behind his ear. A kind of calmness descended on his face.

"Captain Norris," I said, "why don't you take yourself out of here now."

Norris looked from Tanner to me, smiling and shaking his head as if he could not believe what was in front of his eyes.

Tanner drew his revolver from its case. I could feel that motion in my stomach also.

"Sergeant," I said quickly. "Philanthropist is not an insult."

He glanced at me, then back at Norris, and smiled. "Ain't no insult? You wrong, School. Philanthropist mean nigger, doan it, Cap'n?"

He pointed the revolver at Norris. Norris stiffened, then tore open his shirt. He rubbed his filthy chest, pointing to his heart, still swaying.

"Philanthropist," he said.

Tanner cocked the revolver and fired into Norris' chest. Norris flew backwards and fell into a tub that had been sunk into the mud as a latrine. I stood staring at the body, the greenback still clutched in one hand, waiting for him to get up, for the lesson to be over. The flies started gathering quickly; there were many already there. "That was cold murder," I said. But Tanner just smiled at me again, a conspiratorial smile, as if he had seen into my heart, sensed the surge of pure triumph and joy I had felt when he fired into that arrogant breast.

"Bettah," he said.

I open a tent flap, even now, in memory, in dreams, and the prisoners' faces turn to me slowly. A menagerie of the faces of my youth. Even now, in memory, in dreams, they must stay animalistic, for I can't bear think of them as men. Sly, fox-faces. Flat, snake-mean eyes that gleam with contempt, even as they opaque with fear. Bats in a cave, blinking awake. So many eyes. The tents are made to hold sixteen; we stuff in forty. Forty of them: high or low, thick or thin, though they all thinned and sharpened after a while, took on the smudged white and grey coloring of the tents as if they had become a new race. Not foxes nor snakes nor bats. Dogs. A doggish race that we kenneled, their wagging and hand-licking, their nipping at each other, their occasional snarls of defiance, their cur's stink. How they hated me. How I revelled in their hatred. How I hated them back. I raise my Sharps as Tanner had raised his revolver and I point it and I feel the freedom and the power that Tanner must have felt. If they had one head I would blow it off.

I spin around and leave that closed place, seeking air and light. I spin and spin.

Below the prison compound, surrounded by its deadline ditch and stockade, was the Hammond Hospital, a series of twenty buildings arranged like spokes in a circle. Twelve hundred patients could be held in its wards; there were over six thousand when I was at the Point. If the prisoners had become as dogs, then at Hammond the prison surgeons were another race also, a race with serrated, sharpened fingers, with strange hunger in its eyes. Among the Why-dahs, I had read in a book I found once in Dr. Oberle's library, all sickness is thought to come from the curses of enemies: cure came from removing – removing first the curse and then the enemy. To those Whydah, the surgeons of Point Lookout, limbs were curses and their answer was removal also.

It was Tanner who brought me to Hammond, and Tanner of course who took me to the charnel tent, showing it to me like a choice he was putting into my mind, though I did not understand that until later. He pulled back the flap and grinned and stood to one side to let me look. The amputated legs and feet and arms were stacked neatly as cots or tent poles: legs on legs, feet fitted with feet, detached hands cupped, all their palms up. Flesh apple-fresh as stolen youth and flesh already rotted with death, moving with maggots, buzzed by obscenely fat bluebottle flies. Flesh that had blackened or browned, as if our color were contained within it. At the sight of that horrible uniformity my mind tilted and I thought: here they build us.

I fled both the sight and Tanner's laughter and rushed behind the tent. Doubling over, I released a stream of bile, then heaved and retched, my eyes fastened to the ground. Bent over in this posture, I saw the back edge of the tent rise slightly at its bottom, as if being nudged up, and then I screamed, for from that black gap came a scuttling line of detached hands, escaping, scurrying along the ground sideways, their fingers moving like legs. I reeled up and my eyes met Tanner's mocking, red-rimmed orbs. "What sicks you, boy?" he asked, and brought his heel down hard. I heard a terrible, crushing sound. We stood for a moment, our eyes locked, then I looked. Under Tanner's boot, its claws still clutching a trophy of torn flesh, was the good friend of my childhood, a Maryland blue crab, come up from the inlet that lapped near the tent to feast on the grabbers that for so long had pulled his friends and family from the water.

"Come on, School," Tanner said, "got somephin make you feel bettah."

Taking my arm, he led me away from the hospital to a section of the compound to which I had not yet been, to a tent that was identical to all the other tents. He smiled at me and opened the flap just as he had at the charnel tent.

I entered. The flap closing behind me closed me into a dream. A face I had sunken into the deepest depths of myself loosened from its weights and bobbed up, real and inescapable in front of my eyes.

"Private Hallam," Tanner said. "You find somephin you enjoy heah? Pass de time, say? Somephin bettah?"

I nodded, unable to speak.

"Yours," Tanner said simply.

There was no one else in the tent; the others must have been out on work parties. I walked towards the figure on the ground.

"Hallam," I said hoarsely, the sound of my own name in that rank, closed place startling to my ear.

"Hallam," I said again, as if to relieve myself of it, give it back to this skeleton who had given it to me.

He didn't move, only stared at me. If he recognized me, he refused to acknowledge it. As I looked at him, my eyes fastened like crab claws to his flesh, I remembered the day I had marched back into the county and saw it scorched, as if from my wishes. His body was similarly devastated. The powerful form I remembered was wasted away. His hair was mostly gone, except for a few lank, filthy strands. His face was skullish, the skin yellowed and waxy. The padded, sloped strength of his shoulders, the muscles I had seen dancing under a gleam of sweat as he punished, as he hit or drove his need forward into my mother's body, had withered to wing bone. And his hands. These were not the calloused, vein-knotted pinchers I remembered: cunning fasteners and whittlers of wood, boat building hands, trot-lining hands, strokers, graspers, carvers, seizers, twisters, grippers of the handles of whips, of the heavy links of chains, carapaced scuttlers that moved like feeding creatures over the front of my mother's calico dress, patters of warm-waves of love into the top of my head that suddenly grabbed my face, pulled it close as if to a mirror and what he saw in that mirror blossoming on his face into disgust and self-loathing. Those hands.

They had been crushed as if under Sergeant Tanner's boot, the fingers skewed and splintered, black crescent moons where the nails were torn off, the skin as black as the flesh of the hands I had seen pleading at me in the charnel tent, black as if the name he had given me like a curse had come back to him from me. He raised those terrible claws to me. His cracked lips moved and he croaked, but the words were words I might have heard if I had just come into his bedroom of a Sunday morning to help him dress for church:

"Help me, boy."

Did he recognize me? I don't know. Even after I pressed my face to his, even after I called out my name and his crime, screamed it into his face, all he might have seen was another nigger guard calling him to his amount.

I pushed my rage back into my heart, a case that had hardened over the years to contain it.

"You need the hospital," I said.

At the word, a look of horror sprung onto his face. "No," he moaned. "Nooowhooo." It was the howl of a terrified dog.

"You'll die," I said.

"Help me," he whispered, looking into my eyes now as if he at last recognized me. "Feed me," he said.

The slaves in Southern Maryland prepare a ham in a way, my mother told me, that they brought from Africa: it was done both for the tastiness of it and to preserve the meat in hot weather. The negroes would take the pieces of butchered hog their owners would give them on holidays, groove the meat the then stuff the grooves with greens and peppers and mustard seeds. My mother had often prepared this dish for Hallam. It was our old master's favorite meal.

From the guards' garden then, and from some of the traitors that did business in the camp I gathered the ingredients: kale, cabbage, cress, turnip tops and wild onions. The ham I bought from an old negro man in Scotland, just north of the prison: he had lost his family when they were all hurriedly sold to Virginia before the Federal troops came into the area, and he was living with the pig in a little shack outside the abandoned quarters of his master. When I asked him why he didn't move into the main house, he looked at me as if I were a lunatic. He treated that pig with affection, as if it were a child, but he needed the greenbacks and I was willing to pay.

The other guards teased me as I began to prepare the dish, but when they saw my face they stopped and formed a silent circle around me. Silent at first, but after a time they began to mutter, a steady drone of voices that seemed to hum and vibrate in the bone of my skull. " ...His mama...lak the ham...stuff hisself in, split fo sho...wah he do...see, see." I cut the greens and vegetables fine, and I chopped and I chopped, the salty drops of my sweat falling on them and then I put them into a tub, and I mixed in red pepper and salt and mustard seed while all around me and in me the voices droned. I took a clean cotton shirt and I cut it up the front, the guards moaning as the knife touched and split, see, see, and I lay it open on the table. Then I tenderly laid a bed of green on the bloth and turned to the ham. I took my bayonet and cut deep crescents into the pink, giving flesh, making a crisscross pattern, the point of the knife meeting the resistance of the flesh, then my thrust breaking through, the moan around and from me increasing as if all we had passed through that was terrible beyond language had been stripped to this single, gathering sound and it was our word, our language. And I gathered up the greens in my hands, the peppers burning into the small cuts, burning the tender flesh between fingers and nails, and I stuffed that hotness into the holes I had made, pushing them in deep, deep.

I turned the ham over and repeated this process and then I lay it on the bed of green and wrapped it round and tied it shut with twine, the moaning passing lip to lip, reverberating in tremble of my fingers, working that meat. I put the ham on the rack I'd prepared, in a deep pot of water, and I covered it. I boiled it for hours, sitting cross-legged and motionless, sweating. Then I took it from the fire and I let it cool in its own juice for the rest of that night.

In the morning I drained it and I brought it to Hallam.

The other guards followed me at a small distance, and they stood back when I went inside. Hallam's tentmates were still there. They looked up at me with an animalistic dullness from their starved lethargy, their nostrils twitching at the smell of the meat, their mouths salivating.

"Get out," I said.

They stared at me, or rather at the bundle in my hands, transfixed, and I said the words again. As if they were a signal, my companions poured into the tent, screaming my words like echoes, kicking, beating, driving all the prisoners out. All but Hallam.

He lay as I had seen him before, befouled and stinking, his eyes unfocused. I sat down on the earth next to him.

"Hallam," I said, "do you know me?"

His yellowed eyes rolled back in his head. A brownish liquid dribbled down his chin. I seized his jaw between my thumb and forefinger, a gesture remembered by my very skin: the way he would seize me and search my face each time he would see me. His flesh felt rough and hard on its surface but rotten soft underneath, like wood undermined by termites.

"Hallam," I said.

"Hallam," he echoed hollowly.

I laughed. "Yes, Hallam. I bring you something to eat, Hallam. To give you strength. Here." With my free hand, I tore off a chunk of ham. The juice and stuffing clung stickily to my fingers. I pushed it under his nose.

"This is the flesh of your flesh," I said. "Eat of it."

He gagged, his eyes rolling. His hand came up feebly to hold my wrist, but he shrieked when we touched, his rotted fingers bursting and bleeding at the slight contact, as if something in my skin had burned him.

"Eat," I said.

I squeezed my grip until his mouth opened, the stench from the blackened stubs of his teeth and his rotted gums as strong as death. I pushed the ham and greens into that black gap, mashed it into his mouth like a grotesque second tongue. He gagged and swallowed, his eyes rolling. The pink meat mixed with the bile of his insides, his blood; it all spilled out on my hand. Behind him, the other guards watched us silently, a row of grinning heads.

"Hallam," I thought he tried to say.

"Vomit, Hallam," I said. "Vomit Hallam. Vomit me, Hallam."

I pushed more meat into his mouth. He vomited. As if I were floating above myself, drifting up to the apex of the tent, I saw myself, Hallam before Hallam.

I rose and then I knelt and I picked him up. I cradled him in my arms as if he were my child. The bear of a man I remembered was slight, nothing. As we passed outside, the sunlight touched his panicked face and he buried it in my chest. I felt his lips flutter against my skin, as if my heart were beating outside my body.

He only raised his face when the entrance of the hospital suddenly shadowed us. When he looked up and saw where we were, a great cry issued from his lips.

"Noooo. Hallam. Noooo."

"God of Abraham, save us," I whispered into his ear, but I carried him into the darkness, to the dark gods of the Whydah.

It was two days before I could bring myself to go back to the hospital. He lay on his back on the cot, staring up at the ceiling. A bowl of gruel had been placed next to his head, apparently so he could turn his face and lap it like a dog. But either inadvertently or in order to torment him, it had not been placed quite close enough for him to "reach." The gruel was congealing, untouched. A beetle had drowned in its sticky substance.

He stared at me vacantly when I stood over him. He was shrinking into his death, the flesh melting, the skull emerging. I pulled the tattered blanket from him. His yellow flesh had sucked down to the ladder of bones in his chest. His belly was distended with bloat and bristled with a coarse black fur. Tight between his legs, that purse of life, the cursed sac from which unwanted issue was released into the world, was shriveled and black, void of the appearance of flesh. But his arms, down to the stubs of his wrists, lay smooth and innocent at his sides. They weren't horrors, but seemed simply inhuman, mere sticks. Only the stumps themselves looked badly; the surgeon had cauterized clumsily and the flesh there was cracked with bleeding scabs. As I stared, he raised his two arms and brought them together in a strange fashion: the two wrists almost but not quite touching. It took me a moment before what was in his mind emerged as a picture in my own: he was grasping, as if in prayer to me, what was no longer there to grasp: his phantom hands. A prayer, I thought, for forgiveness, but then I saw that his eyes were fastened to that bowl of rancid gruel.

I looked down at him. His passivity, his cringing focus, his utter non-comprehension, suddenly enraged me. Picking up the bowl of gruel, I flung it across the tent. His cauterized wrists waved in its direction helplessly, like the broken antennae of some gigantic, foul insect. Waved at me, as I fled the ward.

I fled, but that night I came back to him. I took him up in my arms and carried him to the ward door. I waited until the sentry had passed, and I carried him outside. He was so light that when I went out into the darkness, I could imagine my arms empty, as if I were carrying smoke. Sergeant Tanner was on duty that night. I had testified in his behalf at the hearing that had been convened after the Norris shooting, a marker I'd called in, though I believe he would have let me do what I wished to do anyway. He imagined I was taking Hallam to finish him. Brother murderer he thought me, though it was murder of which I wished to be relieved. Tanner made sure that no one stopped me, questioned my burden. My burden was light as smoke in my arms and he was the very weight of my life.

I had hidden the skiff under some brush off the Potomac shore and I thought I saw his eyes widen and grow brighter when he saw the water. He was a Hallam, Chesapeake-born; his blood, like mine, run through with estuarine water, that mixture of sea and fresh, the water from the heart of the continent that flushes out its sediment and flows into and dilutes the salt tears of the ocean Passage. A mix of waters that bears and nourishes its own strange, tearing bits of life, species that could not live in the unmixed, pure essence.

I rowed until the shore was a gray seam against the sky, then set the sail. A fog drew around us, and water and sky and time coalesced until I didn't know if we were floating or flying, Hallam and handless Hallam, in a gray ether in which there was only the rasping of his breath, mingling with the groan of canvas, the whistle of wind. If the wind held it would not take me long to get to the other side, and if my luck held as well, I could avoid the Secesh patrols. I knew these waters; I'd fished them for this man's dinner, helped crab and oyster them for my mother's pot. It was a long, wild shore on the Virginia side; I'd leave him on it, one of their patrols would find him. That was my plan. That would have been my plan if I had one, but in truth there was no plan to my voyage, no *logos*, but only a pure and wordless animal need for the relief of weight.

I felt the tick of my heart beat in my palm against the tiller, like an inexorable measure of time. My hands, my skin, my ears all told me I was heading in the right direction, but for all I knew I could have been floating in a fantastical bubble towards the moon. Hallam lay against the bow of the skiff. He raised his face and looked at me through the mist, his face and form, hands gone, wrists wrapped with a breath of smoke, dissolving into that pale opalescent grayness. He smiled. He was fifteen feet from me, at the other end of the boat, but I could feel that smile print like an icy kiss on my lips. He smiled and then he cackled and rolled over the gunnel. I raced to the side and looked over, but all I could see were those two flayed stumps breaking through the mist, their phantom grip squeezing my heart. Then he was gone and I could feel him sinking, sinking, his weight growing heavier inside me as he settled deep.

It was shortly after Hallam's escape that I was transferred from this prison: not because of any suspicion accruing to me from Hallam's disappearance (Tanner had covered me well) but rather because my constant petitions were at last answered. So it was I finally came to the war. And while I was late to the fighting, I saw enough to relegate my memory of Hallam's last days to a small horror, only a comparative (I wanted to believe) by which to measure other horrors. I have seen paralyzed men constantly pinch and prod the flesh of their deadened limbs as if they had to endlessly demonstrate the lack of feeling to themselves. Hallam's pain and death became a vision I touched in just such a manner: only (I told myself) as a test of my numbness. I became, as all good soldiers do, a strange construct without heart or voice, designed only to advance, to aim, to shoot. A pair of feet, a pair of eyes, a pair of hands.

I returned only this far into Southern Maryland: when Father Abraham was murdered by that popinjay of an actor, I was among the troops who hunted him down into Charles County, who followed him over the Potomac. I watched him burn in that Virginia barn, but I felt nothing, neither pity nor delight. All of the fires inside me had already turned to ash.

Afterwards, I rode off by myself, as if to make official the desertion I had taken from my own soul, from lux, years before. I rode north along the river. It was still dangerous country for a black man, particularly one in a blue uniform, but the few whites I saw, furtive and emaciated, looked at me and looked away, afraid of whatever they saw in my eyes, as surely as they feared the rifle slung from my saddle.

I rode until my stomach growled with hunger, and then, as if pulled to the water, I stopped before a dock with most of its planking torn off, but with a skeleton of boards connecting the pilings that marched out into the river.

The dock was off a small meadow; as I rode down to it, I passed the bloated corpse of a cow. I stopped and dismounted. My horse calmly nibbled on the grass near it; like me, he had grown indifferent to carrion. With my bayonet, I sliced off a chunk of the maggoty meat, then cut that into small pieces. The slicing motion of my blade reminded me, for the first time in many months, of the way I had prepared a meal for Hallam. I took a coil of cord from my saddle bag and I fastened the rancid hunks of meat every two feet along the line, using the trot-lining knot Hallam had taught me when I was a small boy, the string looped over itself, each loop tightened like a small noose on the meat. Then I made my way over the framework of boards to the end of the dock, and sat on the small remaining platform of cross boards between the last two pilings. Sat out over that water.

I tied the cord to a piling and threw the end into the river, then I took the slack in my hand, holding it lightly between thumb and forefinger. I had no net or bucket; inasmuch as I thought at all, I thought to pull the crabs out, one by one, and bayonet them. I sat for a long time, dangling my feet, the water flowing around me and from me in a silver stillness. The river pulled the line, as if testing what it had on the other end. Soon I felt the smooth cord begin to tug and jerk harder against my skin, as if it had taken into itself the essence of the life feeding at it, the claws grabbing at the chunks of offal. I began pulling the line slowly in to me, gently so as not to startle the feeding crabs, feeling their slight back tug, the tug between hunger and fear on which we are all strung. Soon I could see one, then two dark shapes growing under the silvery skin of the water, their appendages moving at me like frantic fingers as they broke through the surface.

.....*Wayne Karlin*

The Song of the Word

To my ancestors of the Southern Riverlands of the Chesapeake....
who addressed the right enemy for all the wrong reasons.

At the Battle of Antietam....

They went up to the mountains and crossed Potomac wide.
Captive of the dreams this nation would divide.
In defiance of creation, allied in the absurd,
each song would seek its ending as their flesh became the word.

Kin and kind.....
left their dreams and loves behind.
On a dusty road to glory, in close-ordered ranks conspired
to descend in contradictions, falling ever....reaching higher.
Consumed by word, by water, and by fire!

And to their sons and daughters in all these waters
in this foreground of staging, facing the millennial
battle to sustain and maintain the Chesapeake Creation

May you go up to the mountain, and cross the waters wide.
Become the captain of your dreams and all the songs you hold inside.
May your dream be of creation and of the voice you've heard,
saying: "you are the beginning and the beginning is the word!"

Word will turn!
Turning will conspire!
To reach into the darkness awakening desire,
and arise from contradiction, reaching high, and then go higher.
You are the word, the water, you're the fire!!!

....Tom Wisner

Acknowledgements

Karren LaLonde Alenier's poem, "Looking for Divine Transportation," first appeared in her book, <u>Looking for Divine Transportation</u> (The Bunny and Crocodile Press, 1991), then in <u>Bumper Cars: Gertude Said She Took Him For a Ride</u> (Mica Press). It is reprinted here with permission of the author.

Barri Armatage's poem, "Fitting," first appeared in *The Georgia Review,* and then in <u>Double Helix</u> (Washington Writer's Publishing House) © by the author and reprinted with permission of the author.

Renée Ashley's poem, "Charity," first appeared in *Poetry.* The poem is reprinted with permission of the author.

Ned Balbo's poem, "First Days in a World," appears in his book, <u>Galileo's Banquet</u> (Washington Writers' Publishing House, 1998). The poem is reprinted with permission of the author.

Madison Smartt Bell's story "Dragon's Seed," © 1990 by Madison Smartt Bell, is reprinted here by arrangement with the author, from the collection <u>Barking Man and Other Stories</u>. It was originally published in *Boulevard.*

Jody Bolz's poem, "Shouts of Holy Welcome," first appeared in *The Women's Review of Books* (Wellesley College, 1991) and is reprinted with permission of the poet.

Alan Britt's poem, "Rural Maryland," first appeared in *Folio* and is reprinted here with permission of the poet.

Sterling Brown's poem, "After Winter," appears in <u>The Collected Poems of Sterling A. Brown</u> (Tri-Quarterly Press, 1989) and is reprinted with permission of the poet, to HoCoPoLitSo (1982).

Gilbert Byron's poem, "Evening Marshes," first appeared in <u>These Chesapeake Men</u> (The Driftwood Press, North Montpelier, Vt., 1943). It is reprinted here with permission of Chesapeake College where his papers are housed.

Kenneth Carroll's poem, "Montana Terrace," first appeared in his book, So What (The Bunny and the Crocodile Press, 1997), © retained by the author, reprinted with permission of the author.

Grace Cavalieri's poem, "Blue-Green Spirit," first appeared in Poems, New and Selected (Vision Library Publications, 1994), © retained by the author, reprinted with permission of the author.

Maxine Clair's poem, "Harriet Tubman Said," first appeared in Coping with Gravity (Washington Writer's Publishing House, 1988), © Maxine Clair, reprinted with permission of the author.

Lucille Clifton's poems "blessing of the boats" and "we are running" both appear in quilting (Boa Editions, Ltd., 1991), © retained by the author, reprinted with permission of the author.

Michael Collier's poem, "The Wave," first appeared in his book, The Ledge (Houghton Mifflin), and is reprinted here with permission of the publisher and the author.

Geraldine Connolly's poem, "Lydia," first appeared in *Poetry* and was later published in her book, Food for the Winter (Purdue University Press, 1990), © retained by the author, reprinted with permission of the author.

Sarah Cotterill's poem, "Susan in the Potter's Field," was first published in *Poetry Northwest*. It is reprinted here with permission of the author.

Bruce Curley's poem, "The Kind of Woman to Marry," first appeared in Messages From the Heart. It is reprinted here with permission of the author.

Fred D'Aguiar's poem, "On Duty," first appeared in his book, Mama Dot (Chatto &Windus, 1985). It is reprinted with permission of the author.

Ann Darr's poem, "Flying the Zuni Mountains," is excerpted from "Flying the Zuni Mountains" which appears in her book, Flying the Zuni Mountains (Forest Woods Media Productions, 1994), © Anne Darr, reprinted with permission of the author.

William Heath's poem, "The Forgotten American," first appeared in his book The Walking Man (Icarus Books, Baltimore), © 1994 by William Heath, reprinted with permission of the author.

Barbara Hurd's "The Country Below," first appeared in the *Yale Review* and was then re-printed in The Best American Essays, 1999. It will also be included in her collection of essays, Stirring the Mud: On swamps, boys and the human imagination, forthcoming from Beacon Press. © by the author and reprinted with her permission.

Gray Jacobik's poem, "The Ideal," was first published in *Ploughshares,* 1999 and in The Surface of Last Scattering (Texas Review Press). © Gray Jacobik, reprinted with permission of the author.

Josephine Jacobsen's poem, "Prettyboy Dam," appeared in her book, The Animal Inside (Ohio University Press, 1966) and then in The Sisters: new and selected poems (The Bench Press, 1987). It is reprinted here with permission of the author.

Phil Jason's poem, "Bedtime Story," appeared in *Centennial Review* and then in his book Near the Fire (Dryad Press, 1983). Reprinted with permission of the author.

Rod Jellema's poem, "Why I Never Take Off My Watch at Night," first appeared in *The Plum Review* and is reprinted here with permission of the author.

Lane Jenning's poem, "Stars," was first published in *Wordhouse.* It appears here with the permission of the author.

Dan Johnson's poem, "A House is a Story," first appeared in *Lip Service,* 1992, then in Hungry As We Are (WWPH, 1995). It is reprinted with permission of the author.

Edward P. Jones' story, "Marie," first appeared in *The Paris Review* (1992) and appears in his book, Lost in the City (William Morrow and Company, Inc., 1992). It is reprinted with permission of the author.

Elizabeth Spires' poem, "Thanksgiving Night: St. Michael's," was first published in her book <u>Annonciade</u> (Viking Penguin, 1989), and is reprinted here with permission of the author.

Henry Taylor's poem, "Shapes, Vanishings," © 1986 by Henry Taylor, is reprinted from <u>The Flying Change</u> by permission of the author and Louisiana State University Press.

James Taylor's poem, "Because I Didn't Take The Picture," first appeared in *Puerto Del Sol* and <u>The Anthology of American Political Verse</u>. It is reprinted with permission of the author.

Hilary Tham's poem, "The Thrower of Stones" was first published in the e-zine: *poetrymagazine.com*. It appears here with permission of the author.

Kathy Wagner's poem, "Returning to the City By Boat," was first published in *Southern Poetry Review*. It is reprinted here with permission of the author.

Michael Waters', "The Mystery of Caves," first appeared in *Poetry* and then in <u>Anniversary of the Air</u> (Carnegie Mellon University Press, 1985). It is reprinted with permission of the author.

Julia Wendell's poem, "Fires at Yellowstone," first appeared in *Hayden's Ferry Review* and then in her book <u>Wheeler Lane</u> (Igneus Press, 1998) and is reprinted with permission of the author.

Reed Whittemore's "Still Life" appeared most recently in <u>The Past, The Future, The Present</u> (University of Arkansas Press), © 1990 by Reed Whittemore. His poem, "The Old Trains," first appeared in *Ruby*. Both are reprinted with permission of the author.

Terence Winch's story, "The Rules of Normal Life," first appeared in *Crab Orchard Review* and is reprinted here with permission of the author.

Tom Wisner's lyric "Song of the Word" is published with permission of Tom Wisner, Chesapeake Studios. Music is available from Tom Wisner Studios, Box 7, California, MD 20619; <u>chestory@earthlink.net</u>.

Karen LaLonde Alenier is author of four collections of poetry including her latest, <u>Looking for Divine Transportation</u>. Lincoln College awarded her the first Billie Murray Denny Award for poetry. She is president of The Word Works.

Tyler Anderson was in fourth grade at Park Hall Elementary School in St. Mary's County when he wrote "Lies."

Barri Armitage's Maryland roots go back to the 17th century. She received an M.A. from Syracuse University and now teaches poetry in the Montgomery County public schools.   Her book, <u>Double Helix,</u> won the 1992 Washington Writers' Publishing House Prize.

Renée Ashley's book, <u>SALT</u>, won the Brittingham Prize in Poetry, and her second collection, <u>The Various Reasons of Light</u>, was chosen as the inaugural poetry book for Avocet, Inc. She received a 1997-98 fellowship from the National Endowment of the Arts and her work is included in the Pushcart Prize XXIV.

Ned Balbo holds degrees from Vassar College, the Writing Seminars at Johns Hopkins, and the University of Iowa Writers' Workshop. He teaches at Loyola College in Baltimore and works as an academic dean for the Johns Hopkins Center for Talented Youth. He is currently a literature panelist (arts organizations) for the Maryland State Arts Council

Marguerite Beck-Rex is a writer, water-colorist and performance poet who makes her living as an editor for the Senate Democratic Policy Committee. The mother of two grown sons, she makes her home and her garden in Silver Spring.

J. H. Beall is a physicist and poet who has been a member of the faculty at St. John's College in Annapolis for nearly two decades. He also serves as a senior consultant to the E.O. Hulburt Center for Space Research. His book of poems, <u>Hickey, The Days</u>, was published by The Word Works in 1982.

Madison Smartt Bell is the author of eight novels, two short story collections and a book on writing fiction, <u>Narrative Design</u>. His writing has been nominated for numerous awards and he was named one of the Best Young American Novelists by Granta magazine in 1996. His most recent novel is <u>Ten Indians</u>.

David Bergman is the author or editor of over a dozen books including three volumes of poetry, the latest of which is <u>Heroic Measures</u>. He teaches at Towson State University and lives in Baltimore City and Talbot County.

Judy Bolz lives in Brookmont and teaches creative writing at George Washington University. Her poems have appeared in such publications as *Ploughshares, River Styx,* and *Poet Lore.* In 1998 she received a writer's award from the Rona Jaffe Foundation.

Alan Britt edits and publishes *Black Moon: Poetry of Imagination.* His book, <u>Bodies of Lightning</u>, was published in 1995. He serves as a Maryland State Arts Council Poet-in-the-Schools.

Sterling A Brown was the first Afro-American Poet Laureate. His family owned a farm in Howard County where he spent many summers and holidays between 1911 and the 1940's. He taught at Howard University where he served as mentor for generations of black literary scholars and artists.

Gilbert Byron is often considered the Henry David Thoreau of the eastern shore of Maryland where he lived in a small cabin and observed the Chesapeake life around him. He wrote for over fifty years and died in 1991, three weeks short of his 88th birthday. His cabin/home is now being restored as a memorial to his life and work.

Kenneth Carroll is the D.C. site coordinator for WritersCorps, an arts and social service program founded by the NEA and AmeriCorps. He is past president of the African American Writers Guild. His book, <u>So What! for the white dude who said this ain't poetry</u>, was published in 1997.

Anne Caston graduated from St. Mary's College of Maryland and earned an MFA from Warren Wilson College. Her book, <u>Flying Out With the Wounded,</u> was published by New York University Press in 1997. She served as the Jenny McKean Moore writer in residence at George Washington University and now teaches at the University of Alaska.

Grace Cavalieri, for twenty years the producer and host of WPFW's "The Poet and the Poem," is the author of ten books of poetry. She has written for opera, stage and film. Her awards include a PEN Fiction Award and the Allen Ginsberg Poetry Award. She is presently a writer for West Virginia Pubic Radio, and produces The Poet and the Poem from the Library of Congress.

Adam Chambers was a fourth grade student at Mutual Elementary School in Calvert County when he wrote "Baby Leopard."

Katherine Chandler teaches environmental literature at St. Mary's College, and composition courses that focus on nature and the environment. She also teaches eighteenth and nineteenth century British literature. She is co-author of three young adult novels.

A.V. Christie received her MFA from the University of Maryland at College Park. Her first book of poems, <u>Nine Skies,</u> was a winner in The National Poetry Series Competition in 1996. She has also received a grant from the National Endowment for the Arts.

Maxine Clair lives in Landover. She has degrees from the University of Kansas and The American University. She teaches at George Washington University and her books are <u>Rattlebone</u> and <u>Coping with Gravity.</u>

Lucille Clifton is Distinguished Professor of Humanities at St. Mary's College of Maryland and she holds the Hilda C. Landers Endowed Chair in the Liberal Arts. A former poet Laureate of Maryland, she serves on the board of Chancellors of the Academy of American Poets, and is a Fellow of the American Academy of Arts and Sciences. Her most recent book is <u>Blessing the Boats: New and Selected Poems, 1988-2000.</u>

Dewitt Clinton was in the fourth grade at Park Hall Elementary School when he wrote "I Don't Want To Grow Up."

Jeffrey Lamar Coleman is on the English faculty at St. Mary's College of Maryland, and lives in Huntingtown, with his wife, Ynez. He holds an MFA in Creative Writing from Arizona State University and a Ph.D. in American Studies from the University of New Mexico.

Michael Collier is on the English faculty at the University of Maryland, and directs the Bread Loaf Writer's Conference. He is the author of four books of poetry, most recently The Ledge, published by Houghton, Mifflin. He has received a Guggenheim fellowship and a Pushcart Prize, among other awards.

Geraldine Connolly resides in Montgomery County and teaches at the Writers Center and in the Maryland Poet-in-the-Schools program. She serves as executive editor of *Poet Lore*. Her books include The Red Room, Food for the Winter, and Province of Fire.

Sarah Cotterill received an MFA from the Iowa Writer's Workshop, has been a Yaddo Fellow and has received grants from the Maryland State Arts Council and the NEA. She teaches at the Writers' Center and has published In the Nocturnal Animal House.

Virginia Crawford has a B.F.A. from Emerson and a Master of Letters from the University of St. Andrews in Scotland. She serves as a Poet-in-the-Schools for the Maryland State Arts Council, is co-founder of WordHouse and co-editor of Poetry Baltimore: poems about a city.

Bruce Curley lives in Germantown, Maryland with his wife Robin and sons Joshua, 14 and Eamon, 3. He works as a senior technical writer for DataSource, Inc. and has published in numerous literary journals.

Fred D'Aguiar was raised in Guyana, and currently teaches in the MFA program at the University of Miami. He has written five books of poetry, a play, and three novels, the latest of which is Feeding the Ghosts. His novel, The Longest Memory, won the Whitbread First Novel Award in Great Britain. A memoir of his appeared in *Harper's*.

Ann Darr lives in Bethesda, was an Air Force pilot during World War II and now teaches at American University and the Writer's Center. She has received a Discovery Award and Bunting and NEA Fellowships, has edited several anthologies, including <u>Hungry As We Are,</u> and has published eight collections of poetry, most recently <u>Flying the Zuni Mountains.</u>

Christine Daub lives in Garrett Park, teaches poetry at the Writer's Center and serves as a Maryland Poet-in-the-Schools. She also runs the Plum Writer's Retreat with Geraldine Connolly. She was co-founder and co-editor of *The Plum Review.*

Donna Denizé holds degrees from Stonehill College and Howard University. She has received grants from the Bread Loaf School of English, the D.C. Humanities Council and The Folger Shakespeare Library. She teaches at St. Albans School and has published the book, <u>The Lover's Voice.</u>

Toi Derricotte lived in Maryland for seven years and taught in the Maryland Poets-in-the-Schools program. She received grants from the Maryland State Arts Council and is currently on leave from the University of Pittsburgh to hold the Delta Sigma Theata Distinguished Chair at Xavier University. She is a co-founder of Cave Canem.

Neal Dwyer studied poetry at the University of Nice, France, and George Mason University. He teaches English at Charles County Community College, where he also publishes the *Connections* literary journal. His poems have appeared in *Tar River Poetry* and *The Iowa Review.*

Sara Ebenreck teaches philosophy at St. Mary's College of Maryland. Her interests lie in environmental philosophy, including its relationship to issues of justice and multi-cultural perspectives, women's voices in philosophy, and the intersection of spirituality and philosophy. She was co-founder and editor of the journal, *Earth Ethics.*

Terry Edmonds lives in Columbia, Maryland. He is a Baltimore native who graduated from Morgan State University and who has worked for the Clinton Administration since 1993. He currently serves as a speech writer for the president.

Sister Maura Eichner has spent a lifetime in Maryland, where –until her retirement– she taught in the Department of English at the College of Notre Dame of Maryland. She has published five books of poetry.

Frank Evans has published poems in *The Annapolis Papers*, Poetry at the Angle, *The Baltimore Gay Paper, BOGG*, and *River Styx*. He did medical research in Bethesda, practiced psychiatry in Annapolis, was medical director of a drug dependency program in Baltimore, and most recently has been a sub-investigator at a custom research organization.

Michael Fallon has taught creative writing at UMBC for the last 15 years. The founding editor of the *Maryland Poetry Review*, his first book of poems, A History of the Color Black, was published by Dolphin-Moon Press. His second book is titled, House of Forgotten Names. He lives in Baltimore City with his wife, Ruth.

Roland Flint is currently Poet Laureate of Maryland. Recently retired from Georgetown University where he was honored for his excellence as a teacher, he has several honorary doctorates, and his books have won much national recognition, including the National Poetry Series Award for his collection of poems, Stubborn. His most recent book is Easy.

Elizabeth Follin-Jones' stories, essays, and poetry have appeared in various journals including *Poet Lore, Passager*, and *Maryland Poetry Review*. Her chapbook, One Flight from the Bottom, won the 1990 Artscape poetry Award. She also works in sculpture and has lived in Chevy Chase since 1957.

Sunil Freeman earned a degree in journalism from the University of Maryland. His has published That Would Explain the Violinist, and the chapbook Surreal Freedom Blues. He works at The Writer's Center in Bethesda, Maryland.

Nan Fry has published two books, Relearning the Dark and Say What I Am Called. She received an Individual Artist's Award from the Maryland State Arts Council and has served as a Maryland Poet-in-the-Schools. She also teaches at The Writer's Center.

Martin Galvin recently "untired" after having taught in Maryland schools and colleges for more than pi-cubed years. His poems have recently appeared in Best American Poetry 1997, *Atlantic Monthly, The New Republic,* and *The Christian Science Monitor.*

Maria Mazziotti Gillan is the founder and director of the Poetry Center at Passaic County Community College, editor of the *Paterson Literary Review,* and co-editor of the anthologies, Unsettling America, Identity Lessons and Growing Up Ethnic in America. She has published seven collections of poetry, most recently, Where I Come From: New and Selected Poems.

Eva Glaser was in the fourth grade at Hollywood Elementary School in St. Mary's County when she wrote "Waking."

Michael S. Glaser has taught at St. Mary's College of Maryland for over 30 years. As director of the Annual Ebenezer Cooke Poetry Reading, the Literary Festival at St. Mary's, and the VOICES reading series, he has brought nearly 300 poets and writers to read at the college. In 1995 Glaser received the Columbia Merit Award from the Poetry Committee of the Greater Washington, D.C. area for his service to poetry.

Barbara Goldberg is the author of five books, most recently Marvelous Pursuits. She has received two NEA fellowships and two PEN Syndicated Fiction awards, has served as Poet-in-Residence for Howard County, executive editor for *Poet Lore,* and editor-in-chief for the Word Works. Currently, she is executive speechwriter for AARP.

Judith Hall is the author of To Put The Mouth To, which was selected for the National Poetry Series, and Anatomy Errata, winner of *The Journal* Award in Poetry. She has taught at St. Mary's College of Maryland and is now Poet-in-Residence at California Institute of Technology. She serves as poetry editor of *The Antioch Review.*

Jeffrey Hammond, professor of English at St. Mary's College of Maryland, has published three books on early American literature. His informal essays, one of which won a Pushcart Prize, have appeared or are forthcoming in such periodicals as *Antioch Review*, *The Southern Review*, *Virginia Quarterly Review*, *Shenandoah*, *Crab Orchard Review*, and *The American Scholar*.

Clarinda Harriss chairs the English department at Towson State University. Since the mid-1970's, she had edited and directed BrickHouse Books, Inc., Maryland's oldest small press. The most recently published collections of her poetry are The Night Parrot and License Renewal for the Blind.

Richard Harteis has worked as a physician's assistant, teacher, radio producer and businessman for the Westinghouse Electric Corp. He is the author of five books of poetry, a memoir, Marathon, and, most recently, the novel, Sapphire Dawn - 2005.

William Heath earned a Ph.D. in American Studies from Case Western Reserve University. A writer of both poetry and fiction, he is a professor of English at Mount St. Mary's College. Winner of numerous awards and former editor of the *Monoacy Review*, his most recent novel is The Children Bob Moses Led (Milkweed Editions, 1995).

David Hilton is a professor of English at Anne Arundel Community College. He has published in numerous literary journals and has written six books of poetry, including Huladance and No Relation to the Hotel.

Robin Holland received her M.F.A. in poetry from Vermont College She lives in Edgewater, Maryland, and has published nationally in literary journals. She now teaches cross-genre workshops in creativity and writing in public and private high school programs for visual artists.

Barbara Hurd is a professor of English at Frostburg State University. She co-edits *Nightsun* and directs both the Western Maryland Writers' Workshop and the Mountain Lake Writers' Festival. The recipient of several awards, including the 1994 ARTSCAPE award for Objects in This Mirror, her essay, "The Country Below," appears in the 1999 issue of Best American Essays.

Reuben Jackson works as an archivist with the Smithsonian's Duke Ellington Collection. He writes music reviews for several papers and his poetry has been anthologized in <u>Every Shut Eye Ain't Asleep</u>, <u>Unsettling America</u> and <u>In Search of Color Everywhere</u>. His book, <u>Fingering the Keys</u>, won the 1992 Columbia Book Award.

Gray Jacobik is associate professor of English at Eastern Connecticut State University. Winner of the 1997 Yeats Prize, she is also a recipient of a National Endowment for the Arts Fellowship in Creative Writing. Her most recent books are <u>The Double Task</u> and <u>The Surface of Last Scattering</u>.

Josephine Jacobsen was Poetry Consultant to the Library of Congress from 1971 to 1973. She has published ten books of poetry, two of criticism (with William R. Mueller) four collections of short fiction, and one collected essays, criticism, and lectures. Among her many awards is a fellowship from The Academy of American Poets for service to poetry. Ms. Jacobson has lived in Baltimore for nearly 80 of her 91 years.

Philip K. Jason teaches literature and creative writing at the United States Naval Academy. Among his fifteen books are three volumes of poetry, most recently <u>The Separation</u>. He also writes about modern and contemporary poetry, war literature, and Anais Nin. From 1979-1998, he was editor or co-editor of *Poet Lore*.

Rod Jellema is professor emeritus of English literature at the University of Maryland, where he was founding director of the Creative Writing Program. He has written three books of poems, the latest of which is <u>The Eighth Day: New and Selected Poems</u>, and has received an award for his translations of Frisian poetry.

Lane Jennings is an editor/reviewer by profession, a translator by choice, and a poet by inclination. He lives with his wife, Cheryl, and two pampered cats in Columbia, Md.

Dan Johnson is assistant editor of *The Futurist* magazine in Bethesda, Maryland. His books of poems are <u>Come Looking</u>, <u>Glance West</u>, and <u>Suggestions from the Border</u>.

Jean H. Johnson's book of poems, <u>Forgotten Alphabet</u> was published by Scop Publications. She has been a fellow at the Virginia Center for the Arts and the Jenny McKean Moore seminar at George Washington University.

Edward P. Jones received his MFA in creative writing from the University of Virginia. He has taught writing at American University, George Mason University, University of Maryland, and Princeton University. His short stories are widely published, and his first book, <u>Lost in the City</u>, won the PEN/Hemingway Award for Best First Fiction.

Wayne Karlin teaches at the College of Southern Maryland. Author of five novels and a memoir, he co-edited the landmark anthology <u>The Other Side of Heaven: Postwar Fiction by Vietnamese and American Writers</u>. He has received fellowships from the MSAC, the NEA, and his latest novel, <u>Prisoners</u>, won the 1999 Paterson Prize for Fiction.

Marta Knobloch is the author of three collections of poetry: <u>The Song of What Was Lost</u> (ARTSCAPE Award, 1988), <u>Sky Pond</u> (Columbia Book Award, 1993), and <u>The Room of Months \ La atanza dei mesi</u> (Primio Donna di Ferrara, 1995). Her work has been widely published in the United States and abroad.

Ann B. Knox has published two books of poetry, <u>Stonecrop</u>, and <u>Staying is Nowhere</u>, and a collection of short stories, <u>Late Summer Break.</u>. She lives in a cabin on the first folds of the Appalachians and is a long-time editor of *Antietam Review*.

Danuta E. Kosk-Kosicka writes and translates poetry in English and Polish. By training she is a biochemist. Until June 1997 she was an associate professor in the School of Medicine at Johns Hopkins University and the University of Maryland at Baltimore. Her chapbook <u>Here and There</u> was published in 1999.

Kathryn Lange spent a year with AmeriCorps teaching environmental education for Langley Middle School on Whidbey Island in Puget Sound. She was selected a 1999-2000 Lannan Fellow and served as associate editor of the Maryland Millennial Anthology.

Hiram Larew won the 1999 Artscape award for poetry which resulted in the publication of his chapbook, <u>Part Of</u>. A resident of Upper Marlboro, Hiram is one of the tallest poets writing today.

Dan Laskin is a former journalist who lived in St. Mary's City from 1980 to 1989, working for part of that time as a writer for St. Mary's College of Maryland. Currently, he works as an editor and writer at Kenyon College. He is married and has two sons.

lê thi diem thúy was born in South Vietnam in 1972 during the war. She was raised in Southern California where her family moved after the war ended. Her one-woman show about Vietnam is called *Mua He Do Lua / Red Fiery Summer*.

Barbara F. Lefcowitz has published six books of poetry, a novel, and individual poems, essays, and stories in over 350 journals. She has won writing fellowships from The National Endowment for the Arts, The Rockefeller Foundation, and The Maryland Arts Council, among others. She teaches at Anne Arundel Community College.

Merrill Leffler has been writing about marine science and the Chesapeake Bay since the early '80's. He is a founding member of The Writer's Center in Bethesda and publisher of Dryad Press. His books are <u>Partly Pandemonium, Partly Love</u>; and <u>Take Hold</u>.

Jessica F. Locklear attended the University of Maryland and received her master of arts from the Writing Seminars at The Johns Hopkins University. She works as a graphic artist, both editing and publishing the work of other writers.

Elizabeth Lund received an MFA from Cornell University. She is an editor and poetry reviewer for *The Christian Science Monitor*. Her poems have been widely published, and she has been a finalist for the Brittingham Prize and the Four Way Books Intro Prize. She teaches a poetry workshop at the Framingham Women's Prison in Massachusetts.

Laura Lynds lives in Glen Bernie, Maryland, with her husband, Charles, and daughter Amelia. Teacher, writer and flea market entrepreneur, she is currently homeschooling her daughter and grappling with the "true meaning of housework."

Kathy Mangan teaches writing and literature at Western Maryland College. Her poems have appeared in *The Georgia Review, The Gettysburg Review, Shenandoah, The Southern Review,* and <u>Pushcart Prize XV.</u> A collection of her poems, <u>Above the Tree Line</u>, was published by Carnegie Mellon University Press in 1995.

Anne McCauley was born and raised in southern Maryland, went to college in Connecticut, did an occupational therapy internship in the San Francisco city jail, and returned home where she works as an occupational therapist at St. Mary's Hospital.

Judith McCombs grew up in a geodetic surveyor's family. She has held an NEH fellowship, a Canadian Embassy Senior Fellowship, and a Maryland State Arts Council Award in Poetry. Her most recent poetry books are <u>Against Nature: Wilderness Poems</u> and <u>Territories, Here and Elsewhere</u>.

William Meredith's first book of poems, <u>Love Letter from an Impossible Land</u>, was chosen by Archibald MacLeish in 1944 for the Yale Series of Younger Poets. Since then he has published ten additional collections of poetry, served as Poetry Consultant to the Library of Congress, and won a Pulitzer Prize. His most recent book, <u>Effort at Speech, New and Selected Poems</u>, won the National Book Award for Poetry.

E. Ethelbert Miller is the director of the African American Resource Center at Howard University. Founder of the Ascension Poetry Reading Series, author of six books, including <u>Fathering Words: The Making of an African American Writer</u>, and the editor of three anthologies, his many awards include the O.B. Hardison Jr. Poetry Prize.

Ben Moldover was a junior at Thomas Wooton High School in Montgomery County when he wrote "Depression."

Jean Nordhaus was born in Baltimore. Her books of poetry include <u>My Life in Hiding</u>, <u>A Bracelet of Lies</u>, and <u>A Purchase of Porcelain,</u> about Moses Mendelssohn, which won the 1998 Kinloch Rivers Chapbook Competition.

William Palmer is a professor of English at Alma College in central Michigan where he teaches composition and creative writing. He has published poetry and essays in *Yankee, The Bellingham Review, and Chicago Tribune Magazine.*

Linda Pastan's 10th book of poems, <u>Carnival Evening: New and Selected Poems: 1968-1998</u> was published by Norton and was a finalist for The National Book Award. From 1991-1994 she served as Poet Laureate of Maryland.

Lara Payne grew up in Maryland and attended St. Mary's College of Maryland. She worked as an archeologist and teacher in Southern Maryland and Montgomery county and is currently in the MFA program in creative writing at New York University.

Kathy Pearce-Lewis lives in Bethesda and is an enthusiastic birdwatcher. Her poems have appeared widely in anthologies and magazines.

Maggie Polizos graduated from St. Mary's College of Maryland in 1994. She taught elementary school for several years in Los Angeles and in Washington D.C. and is currently a graduate student of The Johns Hopkins Writing Seminars in Baltimore.

Ilona Popper's poems have appeared in *Antietam Review, Maryland Poetry Review* and *Earth Daughters.* She has performed her poetry in *Excavations: Solos by Three Women Artists,* on Montgomery Cable Television in Maryland.

Jacklyn W. Potter's work appears in several Paper-Mache Press anthologies and in Hungry as We Are: Washington Area Poets (WWPH). For sixteen years, she has directed the Joaquin Miller Poetry Series in Rock Creek Park.

Minnie Bruce Pratt is a widely respected feminist who has received numerous prizes and awards, including a Fulbright Fellowship, a Woodrow Wilson fellowship, and a nomination for the Pulitzer Prize for her five books of poetry, prose, and essays. She teaches as a member of the Graduate Faculty at the Union Institute in New Jersey.

Lia Purpura, a graduate of Oberlin College and The Iowa Writer's Workshop, is the author of The Brighter the Veil. Her collection of essays, Increase, won the AWP Award in nonfiction, and a new collection of her poetry, Stone, Sky, Listing will be published by the Ohio State University Press. She lives in Baltimore and teaches at Loyola College.

dj renegade (Joel Dias-Porter) became a professional disk jockey after leaving the USAF. He has performed his work on the Today Show, as well as in the feature film '*Slam*' which won the Grand Jury Prize at the Sundance Film Festival in 1998.

Marijane Ricketts is a Garret County Greenblood after 30 years of Kensington life and Montgomery County schools. She is a past president of the Writer's League of Washington.

Elisavietta Ritchie's fiction, poetry, creative non-fiction, photographs and translations from Russian and French have appeared in numerous publications including Flying Time: Stories & Half-Stories (1992 & 1996). She has won four PEN Syndicated Fiction awards and has published four other books and four chapbooks.

Kate Richardson taught at Charles Community College for ten years until she became a copywriter. She is a past director of the St. Mary's College Women-In-Poetry Program, and has, since 1980, lived on a farm in Calvert County that her father purchased in 1957.

Charles Rossiter is an NEA fellowship recipient and a widely published poet. He was born in Baltimore and now lives in Oak Park, Illinois. His most recent collection of poetry is Evening Stones.

Marie Robins moved to North Carolina after a career of teaching in Maryland's public schools, but still thinks of herself beside the Potomac in St. Mary's County.

Irene Rouse sells old books on the Internet. Her chapbook <u>Private Mythologies</u> was published in the summer of 1999. She is a contributing editor of *WordWrites!* magazine and a member of *WordWrites!* Traveling Poetry Road Show. In 1998 she received her M.A. in English from Salisbury State University in Maryland.

Larry Rubin received his Ph.D. from Emory University. He has served as a Fulbright Professor of American literature at the University of Bergen, and as a visiting professor at the University of Krakow. He has published four books of poems, most recently, <u>Unanswered Calls.</u>

Karen Sagstetter is editor in chief for the Freer and Sackler Galleries, Smithsonian Institution, and editor of *Asian Art & Culture.* Author of two chapbooks of poetry and two nonfiction books, she won first prize in the fall 1998 Glimmer Train Press short story contest and is the recipient of a grant from the Maryland State Arts Council.

Jane Satterfield's first collection of poems is <u>Shepherdess with an Automatic.</u> A Pushcart Prize nominee for both poetry and the essay, she has an MFA from Iowa's Writer's Workshop, and she lives with her daughter in Baltimore, where she teaches at Loyola College. She also serves as a poetry reviewer for *Antioch Review.*

Diane Scharper is a lifelong resident of Baltimore County and the author or editor of four books, most recently, <u>Song of Myself,</u> a collection of memoirs by college students. She reviews books for the *Philadelphia Inquirer, The New York Times*, and *The Baltimore Sun,* and teaches the writing of memoir at Towson State University.

Sam Schmidt is the co-founder of *WordHouse,* a monthly poetry calendar and literary review for the Baltimore area, and hosts its weekly poetry series at the Minas Gallery. He is a recipient of a Maryland State Arts Council Grant and works for John Hopkins University Press.

Aurelie Sheehan is the author of the short story collection <u>Jack Kerouac Is</u> <u>Pregnant</u>. Her poetry and prose have been published in many literary magazines, and she has been anthologized in <u>The Pushcart Prize XXIII: Best of the</u> <u>Small Presses 1999</u>. She is the poetry and lectures coordinator at the Folger Shakespeare Library in Washington, D.C.

Edgar Silex holds an M.F.A. from the University of Maryland. He is the author of <u>Through All The Displacements</u>, and a chapbook, <u>Even The</u> <u>Dead Have Memories.</u> He has received fellowships from the NEA and the Maryland State Arts Council, and was the director of the Baltimore Literary Center, teaching creative writing and Native American mythology.

Myra Sklarew was born and raised in Baltimore and learned to love reading at the Enoch Pratt Library. She teaches at The American University and has written poetry, fiction, essays, and science articles.

Tracy Slaughter was in the sixth grade at Fallston Middle School in Harford County, Maryland when she wrote "Minnow."

Rose Solari is a poet, playwright, and fiction writer. Her chapbook, <u>The</u> <u>Stolen World</u>, won the 1993 Artscape Prize, and her book, <u>Difficult Weather</u>, was selected for the 1995 Columbia Prize for Poetry. Her recognitions include a University Prize from the A.A.P. and grants from the D.C. Commission on the Arts and Humanities and the M.S.A.C. Her most recent publication is <u>Selections: Myths & Elegies</u>.

Elizabeth Spires lives in Baltimore and is a professor of English at Goucher College where she holds a Chair for Distinguished Achievement. She is the author of four books of poems: <u>Globe</u>, <u>Swan's Island</u>, <u>Annonciade</u>, and <u>Worldling,</u> and three books for children, <u>The Mouse of Amherst</u>, <u>With One</u> <u>White Wing</u>, and <u>Riddle Road.</u>

Robert Strott was born in Bethesda and attended St. Mary's College of Maryland. He has been an annual participant in the Literary Festival there since 1990; he considers it a pilgrimage.

Henry Taylor received the Pulitzer Prize in 1986 for his third collection of poetry, <u>The Flying Change.</u> He is professor of literature and co-director of the MFA Program in Creative Writing at American University in Washington, D.C.

James Taylor is the founder and president of Dolphin-Moon Press and a graduate of the University of Maryland and Johns Hopkins Writing Seminars. He has published three books of his own work and is also founder of the American Dime Museum.

Hilary Tham is the author of five books of poetry and a memoir. She has taught creative writing in Montgomery County, was HoCoPoLitSo's Visiting Poet to Howard County, and has been featured several times on cable TV. She teaches for the Writer's Center and is poetry editor of the *Potomac Review*.

Stacy Tuthill is the author of three collections of poems: <u>House of Change</u>, <u>Necessary Madness,</u> and <u>Pennyroyal</u>. She is also the author of <u>The Taste of Smoke: Stories About Africa</u>, and was a PEN Syndicated Fiction Winner. She has edited several anthologies, and is founding editor and publisher of Scop Publications.

Jeanne Fryberger Vote, as director of Continuing Education at St. Mary's College of Maryland, has co-organized and participated in two study tours to Guatemala. She plays the harpsichord in the Maryland Bach Aria Group and directs the music at Historic Trinity Church in St. Mary's City.

Kathy Wagner was born in Baltimore and currently serves as an assistant professor of English at Washington College where she teaches creative writing, 20th century American literarture, and serves as director of gender studies. She lives in Chestertown, Md.

Michael Waters teaches at Salisbury State University. Recent publication includes <u>New and Selected Poems</u> (BOA Editions), and inclusion in the 7th edition of <u>Contemporary American Poetry</u>.

Lauri Watkins came from New York to Maryland where she was nurtured by the rivers of St. Mary's County and earned a B.A. from St. Mary's College. She is currently residing in Seattle.

Julie Wendell lives and works on a horse farm in Upperco. Her most recent collection of poems, <u>Wheeler Lane</u>, appeared from Igneus Press in 1998.

Bernard Welt is the humanities coordinator and an associate professor in the Department of Academic Studies at The Corcoran School of Art where he teaches interdisciplinary humanities courses and cinema. He is the author of two books of poetry, <u>Serenade</u> and <u>Wave</u>, and <u>Mythomania: Fables, Fantasies and Sheer Lies in American Popular Art.</u>

Reed Whittemore is a former Poet Laureate of Maryland as well as a former Poetry Consultant for the Library of Congress. He is a professor emeritus at the University of Maryland where he taught from 1967-1984. His most recent book is <u>The Past, The Future, The Present</u> (University of Arkansas Press, 1990).

Terence Winch has published two books of poems, a collection of short stories, and has contributed to many anthologies and publications. He plays and records traditional Irish music primarily with the band Celtic Thunder, which he started with his brother in 1977.

Tom Wisner creates and records music specifically about Chesapeake waters and culture. <u>Chesapeake Born</u> and <u>We've Got to Come Full Circle</u>, his two earlier recordings, are now housed in the Smithsonian Folkways collection. A new CD of his Chesapeake music will be out in Spring 2000 from <u>chestory@earthlink.net</u>.

Brian Wood was a sophomore at Leonardtown High School in St. Mary's County when he wrote "my diRtY SaVIoR."

Karen Zealand is a counseling therapist and has been in private practice with her psychologist husband in Cumberland, Md. for over 15 years. She is co-editor of *Nightsun*, a literary journal published through Frostburg State University.